A New Map Of The River Thames From Oxford To London, From Entirely New Surveys, Taken During The Summer Of 1871

Gough Adds Gen: Top: 4° 6²

Second]

. A NEW MAP

OF

THE RIVER THAME

FROM

OXFORD TO LONDON,

FROM ENTIRELY NEW SURVEYS, TAKEN DURING THE SUMMER

WITH A GUIDE, GIVING EVERY. INFORMATION REQUIRED BY THE TOURIST, THE OARSMAN,

By HENRY W. TAUNT,

PHOTOGRAPHER (BY APPOINTMENT) TO THE OXFORD ARCHITECTURAL SOCIET

ILLUSTRATED WITH EIGHTY PHOTOGRA

OXFORD: HENRY W. TAUNT, 33, CORNMARKET-STREET.

Corrected to]
[*Entered at Stationers' Hall.*]

PREFACE TO THE SECOND EDITIO[N]

OWING to the rapid sale of the first impression,—the whole of the copies bei[ng]
. in six weeks from the day of publication,—prompted also by many other 'tc[ken]
with which my work has been received, I have minutely revised the "Guide," pre[vious to]
re-issue. The details, therefore, may be relied on as current, the additional precau[tion of a]
journey down the river having been taken expressly to secure the most accurate in[formation;]
the sites of a number of the hotels have been added to the engraved plates, wit[h other]
useful items.

I have been requested to bring out, on a corresponding scale, a Map of the [country round]
Oxford; and, having by me nearly all the requisite *materiel*, I should be happy t[o issue a com-]
panion "Guide," if favoured with the names of a fair number of subscribers (say 200)[, to ensure]
that the necessary cost and labour of such a compilation would not be mi[sincurred. The]
navigation of the upper stream is in a fair way of being much improved; and th[us]
a boating excursion westward may soon become a thing of the past.

OXFORD,
April, 1873.

PREFACE TO THE FIRST EDITION

I T has been justly observed by some writer, that the most lengthy of recommer might easily be reduced to the simple sentence, "Read my Book." The my first attempt at acquaintance with the public through the medium of the " wish to condense my introductory remarks. Let me, however, in this form a courtesy of friends, with whose aid the "Guide" has been so far completed :— Fennell, for his humorous article on "Fishermen," as well as the valuable am description he has furnished ; to R. W. S., for his "Camping Out ;" to Mr. Stanf cross, and his employées, for the splendid manner in which they have carried c and last, but not least, to my old friend Mr. James Williams, of Cirencester, fc in undertaking the general revision of the work,—I here offer my sincere and Nor will I forget those persons on the river who have supplied me with inform; but hope, for the sake of "auld lang syne," to see them in the leisure hours tha admit of.

The idea of a Thames Map, with necessary local information, first suggest from my finding, personally, the need of such a thing. Originally, I proposed a map of the river from its source at Trewsbury Mead to Putney, upon a sc to a mile ; and, in the intervals of photographing, surveyed the greater part o but, finding that, where islands lay in the stream, or the way was barred by l it would be impossible, on so small a scale, to give accurate detail, only that porti below Oxford has been brought out ; but on a scale of *two* inches to the mile.

The measurements given were carefully chained along the towing-path ban and represent the distance a person would walk who was towing a boat.

OXFORD,
June 1, 1872.

INDEX.

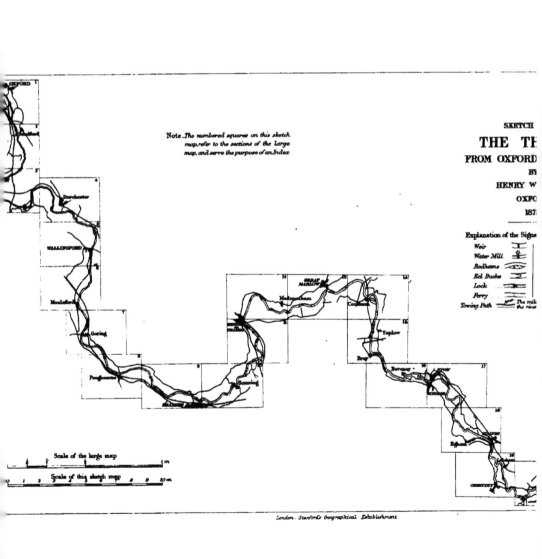

Note._The numbered squares on this sketch
map, refer to the sections of the Large
map, and serve the purpose of an Index

SKETCH

THE TH

FROM OXFORD

BY

HENRY W

OXFO

187

Explanation of the Signs

Weir
Water Mill
Rodhams
Eel Bucks
Lock
Ferry
Towing Path   The mile
                     the rive

OXFORD

Dorchester

WALLINGFORD

Moulsford

Goring

GREAT MARLOW

Medmenham

Cookham

Taplow

Bray

Boveney

Pangbourne

Sonning

Eton

Egham

CHERTSEY

Scale of the large map   1 m.

Scale of this sketch map   5   10 m.
0   1   2

London. Stanford's Geographical Establishment

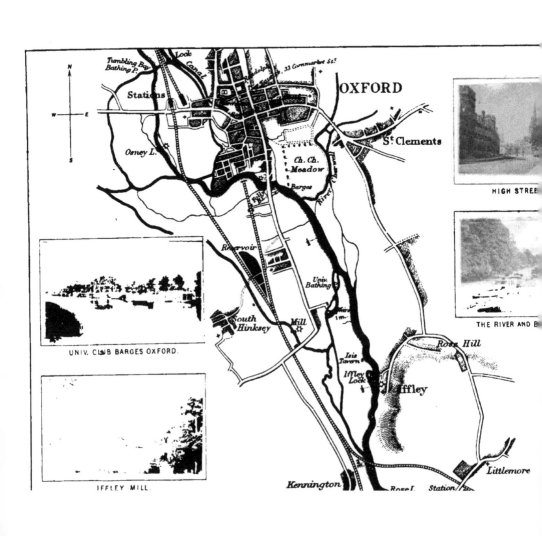

Tumbling Bay
Bathing P.
Lock
Canal
Stations
Randolph
33 Cornmarket St
OXFORD
Osney L.
St Clements
W
N
S
E
Ch. Ch.
Meadow
Barges
River
HIGH STREE
Reservoir
Univ.
Bathing
THE RIVER AND B
South
Hinksey
Mill
Rose Hill
UNIV. CLUB BARGES OXFORD.
Isis
Tavern
Iffley
Lock
Iffley
IFFLEY MILL.
Kennington
Rose L.
Station
Littlemore

OXFORD.

It would be impossible to give, within the limited space of this work, any detailed account of the City of Oxford and its colleges:—tourists who wish to see its beauties, may easily do so under the guidance of one among the men whose business it is to shew the "lions" of the place, or with the aid of books that are published on the subject, a list of which is subjoined.

Oxford should be seen during the "Commemoration Week," which recurs annually in June:—then, throughout the city, and on the river, pleasure is the order of the day, and everything wears holiday garb. In the gay barges lining the beautiful banks of Christ Church walk, enlivened by the varied costumes of many oarsmen, the river has, at Oxford, charms which it can boast nowhere else.

Leaving Oxford we come to Iffley:—close below the lock is a picturesque mill. The Church, which stands on the hill just above, can be seen from the river: it will repay a visit, being a splendid specimen of late Norman Architecture. Rose Island a little farther on, with its picturesque inn, was introduced in the play of "Formosa."

Guides to Oxford.

"**Guides and Views of Oxford,**" sold by **HENRY W. TAUNT, 33, Cornmarket-street,** (marked by red spot on Plan). See inside Cover.

Heywood's "Penny Guide," (with Plan 2d., and with Map 3d.)
Parker's "Railway Traveller's Walk through Oxford." 1s.
Parker's "Handbook to Oxford." 12s.
Shrimpton's "Guides." 1s., 2s., 5s., 7s. 6d.

Oxford. Folly Bridge Lock, from Oxford 0 m.; from Putney, 104 m. 3 fur. 66 yds.; (to Iffley, 1 m. 3 fur. 150 yds.;) is open in high-water times; in summer falls from 1 ft. 6 in. to 2 feet.

Iffley Lock, from Oxford (Folly Bridge) 1 m. 3 fur. 150 yds.; to Sandford Lock, 1 m. 5 fur. 70 yds.; average fall, about 2 ft. 6 in.; does not vary much.

Boats to be let or hou
Those marked * are boat-bu

* J. and S. Salter, Folly Bridge, and at tl
* J. Clasper, Isis-street. (See p. 59.)
* Geo. West, St. Aldate's-street, and B.N
* R. Talboys.
  W. Bossom, (Punts only).

HOTELS.

The "Roebuck," Cornmarket-street. (Se
The "Randolph," Beaumont-street.
The "Clarendon," Cornmarket-street.
The "Maidenhead," Turl-street, and oth

INNS.

The "Crown and Thistle," Market-street
The "Plough," Cornmarket-street. (See
The "Ship," Ship-street, and others.

Fishing.—Fishing at Oxford is of a very except that in the water belonging to the This is caused partly by the amount of plea of the river, and partly by the fact that t severely netted in former years as to leave angler's rod. Below Iffley Lock however and, under the care of the new bye-laws servancy, and their experienced officer, (may hope for better days, when a fair d a fair day's trial.

FISHERMEN.

T. Such, St. Aldate's; W. Bossom, Medl

Fish.—Pike, Perch, Tench, Roach, Dac

Bathing—Parson's Pleasure, at the back Tumbling Bay, near the Botley Road.
New University, at the Long Bridges.

Library—There is a fine Public Library (Hall, in St. Aldate's-street.

DISTANCES.

	From Oxford (Folly Bridge).			From London (Putney Bridge).			From Place to Place.			
	m.	fur.	yds.	m.	fur.	yds.	m.	fur.	yds.	
Oxford Bridge .	0	0	0	104	3	66	0	0	0	Oxford Bridge to Iffley Lock
Iffley Lock .	1	3	150	102	7	136	1	3	150	Iffley Lock to Rose Island
Rose Island .	2	2	54	102	1	12	0	6	124	Rose Island to Sandford Lock
Sandford Lock .	3	1	0	101	2	66	0	6	166	Sandford Lock to Nuneham Bridge
Nuneham Bridge	5	6	160	98	4	126	2	5	160	Nuneham Bridge to Abingdon Lock
Abingdon Lock .	7	6	0	96	5	66	1	7	60	Abingdon Lock to Abingdon Bridge
—— Bridge .	8	1	211	96	1	75	0	3	211	Abingdon Bridge to Culham Lock
Culham Lock .	10	1	211	94	1	75	2	0	0	Culham Lock to Appleford Rail^y Bridge
Appleford Railway Bridge	11	4	67	92	6	219	1	2	76	Appleford Rail^y Bridge to Clifton Lock
Clifton Lock .	13	0	121	91	2	165	1	4	54	Clifton Lock to Clifton Bridge
—— Bridge .	13	4	41	90	7	25	0	3	140	Clifton Bridge to Day's Lock
Day's Lock .	16	0	81	88	2	205	2	4	40	Day's Lock to Junct. of River Thame
Junction of River Thame	16	7	41	87	4	25	0	6	180	Junct. of River Thame to Keen Edge Ferry
Keen Edge Ferry	17	7	181	86	3	105	1	0	140	Keen Edge Ferry to Shillingford Bridge
Shillingford Bridge .	18	6	61	85	5	5	0	6	100	Shillingford Bridge to Benson Lock
Benson Lock .	20	0	91	84	2	195	1	2	30	Benson Lock to Wallingford Bridge
Wallingford Bridge .	21	2	91	83	0	195	1	2	0	Wallingford Bridge to Nuneham Ferry
Nuneham Ferry .	21	6	161	82	4	125	0	4	70	Nuneham Ferry to Stoke Ferry
Stoke Ferry .	23	7	161	80	3	125	2	1	0	Stoke Ferry to Moulsford Rail^y Bridge
Moulsford Railway Bridge	24	4	207	79	6	79	0	5	46	Moulsford Rail^y Bridge to Moulsford Ferry
Moulsford Ferry .	25	2	51	79	1	15	0	5	64	Moulsford Ferry to Cleeve Lock
Cleeve Lock .	26	4	129	77	6	157	1	2	78	Cleeve Lock to Goring Lock
Goring Lock .	27	1	129	77	1	157	0	5	0	Goring Lock to Basildon Rail^y Bridge
Basildon Railway Bridge	28	3	190	75	7	96	1	2	61	Basildon Rail^y Bridge to Gate-Hampton Ferry
Gate-Hampton Ferry	28	6	36	75	5	30	0	2	66	Gate-Hampton Ferry to Whitchurch Lock
Whitchurch Lock .	31	2	69	73	0	217	2	4	33	Whitchurch Lock to Mapledurham Lock
Mapledurham Lock	33	4	139	70	6	147	2	2	70	Mapledurham Lock to The "Roebuck"

Hurley Lock .	52	6	102	1	4	184	51	4	168	Hurley Lock to Hurley Lock
Temple Lock .	53	3	125	7	161	0	50	5	23	Temple Lock to Temple Lock
Marlow Bridge .	54	7	106	3	180	1	49	3	201	Marlow Bridge to Marlow Bridge
— Lock .	55	0	213	2	73	0	49	1	107	— Lock to Marlow Lock
Spade Oak Ferry .	57	1	198	88	2	0	47	1	205	Spade Oak Ferry to Spade Oak Ferry
Cookham Bridge .	58	7	44	4	22	1	45	5	66	Cookham Bridge to Cookham Bridge
— Lower Ferry .	59	3	154	7	132	0	44	4	110	— Lower Ferry to Cookham Lower Ferry
Cleveden Ferry .	59	6	198	4	88	0	44	3	44	Cleveden Ferry to Cleveden Ferry
Boulter's Lock .	61	2	156	0	130	1	43	3	178	Boulter's Lock to Boulter's Lock
Maidenhead Bridge .	62	0	6	3	60	0	42	5	70	Maidenhead Bridge to Maidenhead Bridge
Bray Lock .	63	3	158	7	128	1	40	3	152	Bray Lock to Bray Lock
Monkey Island .	64	0	66	3	0	0	40	4	128	Monkey Island to Monkey Island
Boveney Lock .	66	5	66	6	0	2	37	5	0	Boveney Lock to Boveney Lock
Windsor Bridge .	68	4	156	6	130	1	35	7	90	Windsor Bridge to Windsor Bridge
Romney Lock .	69	0	32	3	34	0	35	3	96	Romney Lock to Romney Lock
Victoria Bridge .	69	6	66	5	0	0	34	5	34	Victoria Bridge to Victoria Bridge
Albert Bridge .	71	1	72	2	214	1	33	3	6	Albert Bridge to Albert Bridge
Old Windsor Lock .	72	0	66	3	0	0	32	6	214	Old Windsor Lock to Old Windsor Lock
Magna Charta Island .	73	3	66	0	0	1	31	3	0	Magna Charta Island to Magna Charta Island
Bell Weir Lock .	74	7	3	4	63	1	29	3	157	Bell Weir Lock to Bell Weir Lock
Staines Bridge .	75	6	198	4	88	0	28	7	195	Staines Bridge to Staines Bridge
Penton Hook Lock .	77	5	146	5	140	1	26	6	168	Penton Hook Lock to Penton Hook Lock
Laleham Ferry .	78	4	66	7	0	0	25	6	140	Laleham Ferry to Laleham Ferry
Chertsey Lock .	79	5	70	5	216	1	24	1	4	Chertsey Lock to Chertsey Lock
Shepperton Lock .	81	5	33	6	33	1	22	7	183	Shepperton Lock to Shepperton Lock
Halliford Point .	82	7	66	4	0	1	21	2	33	Halliford Point to Halliford Point
Walton Bridge .	83	6	2	5	64	0	20	6	156	Walton Bridge to Walton Bridge
Sunbury Lock .	85	3	132	7	154	1	18	5	130	Sunbury Lock to Sunbury Lock
Hampton Ferry .	87	4	22	7	44	2	16	0	110	Hampton Ferry to Hampton Ferry
Moulsey Lock .	88	2	132	0	154	0	16	6	110	Moulsey Lock to Moulsey Lock

SANDFORD.

SANDFORD LOCK, from Iffley Lock, 1 m. 5 fur. 70 yds. ; to Nuneham Bridge, 2 m. 5 fur. 160 yds. : falls from 4 ft. 6 in. in high to 7 ft. 6 in. in low water ; average in summer about 6 feet.

Inn at Sandford, "The King's Arms."

The pools at Sandford are pretty, but very dangerous for bathers ; the large one, having an obelisk to the memory of two Christ Church men who were drowned whilst bathing here, has a certain amount of interest attached to it. Below, as we near Nuneham, the wooded hills make a fine background to the river ; and along the edge of the reedy flams which line its left bank are fine spots for jack and other fish. This is the fishing-ground for anglers from Oxford ; and for a long distance spots may be chosen that will repay a pitch.

NUNEHAM.

*** NUNEHAM BRIDGE. *The middle arch of this bridge must be avoided, on account of the extreme shallowness of the water under it.*

NUNEHAM, the seat of the Harcourt family, the favourite gathering-place for pic-nic parties from Oxford, is one of the prettiest spots on the whole of the river. The park, which contains about 1,200 acres, extends along the Oxfordshire bank of the river for some distance ; it is finely varied with beautiful rolling slopes, rising from the margin of the water, and in places where the waving foliage of its overhanging trees are mirrored in the silvery Thames, it forms a tableau only surpassed by Cleveden itself. The house is situate on the brow of the hill, a short dis-

tance from the river, and is in the Italia chief attraction to the very beautiful garde were considered almost unrivalled.

Amongst their best features at the present the Rock Grotto with the Orangery and R of the terrace ; and amongst minor beautie: walk leading to Whitehead's Oak, where, fine views which present themselves, the c conduit with the foreground and distant pleasing. This old structure once stood o still bears that name. It was presented by Earl Harcourt, who removed it to its pre a picturesque object in itself, and is v account, as well as for the distant views s the hill on which it stands ; in one directior peeping out from amongst the trees, the closed by the range of Chilterns, finishin whilst to the north the spires and towers o relief against the rich background of the Bl

But the loveliest views at Nuneham are where pleasure-parties land : the rustic cot sylvan shade, and the picturesque bridge cr with the whole picture of still life reproduc below, form a series of beautiful picture: can produce.

By previous application by letter to the : number of party, &c., permission can be parties to land on Tuesdays or Fridays, a the cottages if required.

ABINGDON JUNCTION STATION (G. W. R.) from Nuneham, on right bank. The line fr continued to Radley, a mile nearer Oxf Abingdon Junction Station will be done aw

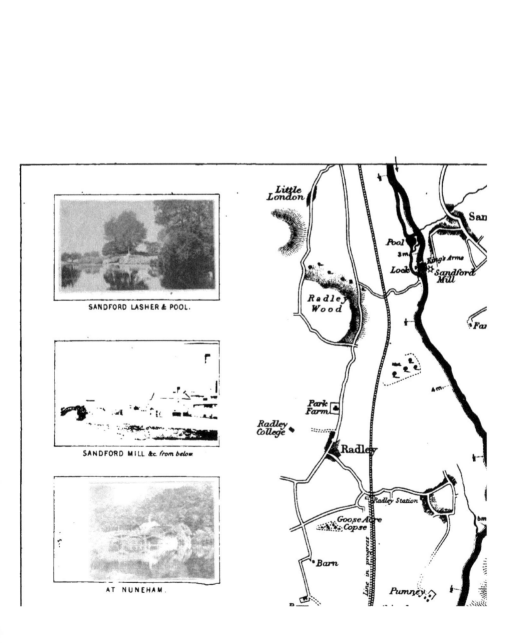

SANDFORD LASHER & POOL.

SANDFORD MILL &c. *from below.*

AT NUNEHAM.

Little
London

San

Pool

3 m.

Look

King's Arms

Sandford
Mill

Radley
Wood

Fa

4 m.

Park
Farm

Radley
College

Radley

Goose Acre
Copse

Radley Station

Barn

Line in progress

Pumney

ABINGDON
Station
Lock
Thrup
Carfax
Cottages
6m.
Wood
Park
8m.
Rivy Farm
Overfall
7m.
R. Ock
Canal
Old River
9m.
Culham College
Clifton
Hampden
Culham Station
Culham
Clifton Farm
Locks
10m.
11m.
Sutton Pool
Mill
Sutton Courtney
12m.
Appleford

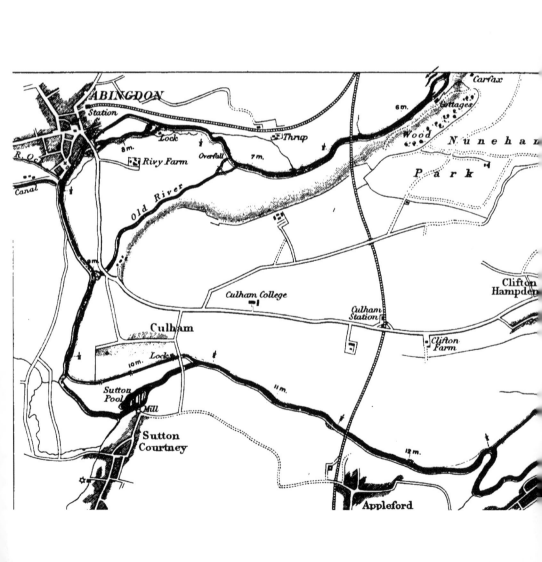

ABINGDON.

Abingdon Lock, from Nuneham Bridge, 1 m. 7 fur. 60 yds. ; to Abingdon Bridge, 3 fur. 211 yds. : falls from 5 ft. in high to 7 ft. in low water ; average in summer, about 6 ft.

Abingdon Bridge, from Oxford, 8 m. 1 fur. 211 yds. ; to Culham Lock, 2 m.

Abingdon. Railway Station, Stert-street (G. W. R. Branch).

Abingdon is a very old town, and contains some curious remains. The most noticeable are,—St. Nicholas and St. Helen's Churches, the Abbey Gateway, and the Almshouses. St. Nicholas Church stands in the Market-place, and is very ancient, the lower part of it being in the Norman style ; it joins the old gateway which once belonged to the abbey. St. Helen's Church stands close to the river, its spire being a conspicuous object, both up and down, for some distance ; it is now undergoing considerable restoration. The Almshouses form the boundary of the churchyard on two sides ; one of the buildings is a curious timber structure with cloisters, and on its front are several rude paintings. There are others also on the end facing the river, including one of the celebrated Abingdon Cross, destroyed by Waller's soldiers. On the north side of the town is a new pleasure park, with a handsome memorial to Prince Albert. Hyde and Clarke's wholesale clothing manufactory, giving employ indoors and out to several thousands of hands, is well worth a visit ; also the new Grammar School, if time will permit. The Wilts and Berks Canal joins the Thames here, the entrance being on the right bank of the river, a short distance below St. Helen's Church. It joins the Kennett and Avon Canal below Devizes, leading to Bath and the lower part of the Severn ; and also, by a branch on the right before reaching Swindon, communicates with the Thames and Severn Canal near Cricklade, whence the Severn, the Warwickshire Avon, or the upper part of the Thames, can be reached. The canal is in very bad order in places, but is well worth the angler's exploration.

Boats to be let and ho

*Blake (at Abingdon Lock).
Hall, the "Anchor" (near St. Helen's Cl
Boats are also housed at the "Nag's Hea

HOTELS.

The "Crown and Thistle," near the bridg
Landing, at the "Nag's Head," on
The "Queen's," in the Market-place.
Landing-stage at the "Anchor," nea

INNS.

The "Nag's Head."
The "Anchor."

Fishing.—The fishing above Abingdon t Near Abingdon Bridge is a sharp stream, for Dace, &c. ; and at Blake's Pool are Chul the Lock the water is deep, and affords fine Cottages at Nuneham, close above which swims.

Below Abingdon, to the Culham Cut, the except in places, which are easily detected b

FISHERMEN.

Jem Short (commonly called "Splash"),
Ambrose Keats, West St. Helen's-street.
Sam Taylor.
Charles Trinder.

Fish.—Pike, Tench, Perch, Dace, Chub,

Bathing at the Weir—belonging to the Ab (*Secretary*—Mr. Leverett, Bath-street).

H. W. TAUNT'S Agent at Abingdon : Mr. HUGHES,

THE THAMES ABOVE OXFORD.

BY THE EDITOR.

LEAVING Folly Bridge, winding along the river past the Oxford Gas-works, and passing under the line of the G. W. R., we soon come to Osney Lock (falls 2 ft. 6 in.), close by which was the once-famous Abbey. There is nothing left to attest its former magnificence and arrest our progress, so we soon come to Botley Bridge, over which passes the western road from Oxford to Cheltenham, Bath, &c. ; and a little higher are four streams, the bathing-place of "Tumbling bay" being on the westward one. Keeping straight on, Medley Weir is reached (falls 2 ft.), and then a long stretch of shallow water succeeds, until we reach Godstow Lock.

Godstow Lock (falls 3 ft. 6 in., pay at Medley Weir) has been rebuilt, and the cut above deepened, the weeds and mud banks cleared out, so as to leave the river good and navigable up to King's Weir. Just above here, you pass close to the ruins of the Nunnery, celebrated from its connection with Fair Rosamond, who lived and died here. The buildings were destroyed by fire in the reign of Charles II., and only the ruins of the chapter-house, with the crumbling walls, give witness of their former extent. Close by is the "Trout" Inn.

King's Weir, a mile above, (falls 3 ft.), has been repaired and re-opened, but is still one of the most awkward weirs to get through on the river, and it is much wiser, if possible, to pull your boat over at that place. There is a talk of making a new pound-lock in place of the weir, but whether it will come off remains to be seen; if it does, it will do more for the pleasure-navigation of the upper part of the river than any other thing I know. After King's Weir, we pass nothing worth notice till nearly at Eynsham, just before reaching which the Thames is joined by the Evenlode. The woods are pretty, and the banks

of the river are broken, but there is nothin magnificent scenery of a few miles below.

Eynsham Weir is our next ; it falls abou but in winter all the weirs on the upper 1 Tredwell, at the Lock-house close to the Pinkle (the next Lock) open for you, or here, will take charge of your boat, &c. "Red Lion."

After Eynsham Bridge is passed, for th the windings of the river appear like the serpent ; in places nearly doubling on itsel full twice what it otherwise would be : ther and you are just a mile from Skinner's Wei

Skinner's Weir is one of those quaint o that artists love. It has been in the occu from father to son, for a long number of y to get a glass of beer here, but no beds Skinner will be, if you like originality, ; Harcourt is only a little distance across t the church and Pope's tower is well repaid

Bablock Hythe Ferry and Inn (no be reached. Close here is "Cumnor," mad Scott's "Kenilworth ;" and also "The D stones reared in a field, supposed to comm in Saxon times ; and then nothing is mo Ridge's Weir (falls 1 ft. 6 in.) ; one bed. to keep the house is gone to her rest ; but

Half a mile above is *New*bridge, the o Inn stands close to the bridge, but the rec

you may be accommodated, or you may be told there is nothing nearer than Standlake, two miles off. The Windrush joins just close above the bridge; and a little further on you will find the river grown up with water-parsley; but it is not so bad as it was a summer or two ago, before Mr. Campbell's barges went up and down from Buscot: however, it is quite bad enough, even now there is a certain amount of traffic. Shifford lies on the left bank. It was a meeting-place for a kind of parliament in the reign of Alfred, and was then no doubt a place of importance; but a little church and a few houses are all that are left. Do not omit to take the left-hand stream going up, both by the island below and also just by Shifford. The weirs above Ridge's are all gone; some washed away, and the rest pulled out by the Conservators.

Duxford Weir, next above, was rather picturesque, and there are some very pretty glimpses both at the ferry and in the village. The scenery all along this part of the Thames is very flat, and generally uninteresting; but now and then some sweet spots are passed, that seem even more so from the contrast with the uninteresting scenery around. Duxford Farm, and the landing-place to the ferry, are instances; but they hardly repay one for the dreary stretch of river that reaches to Tadpole Bridge, with only one break (Ten-foot) between. An Inn, with beds, at Tadpole Bridge; nothing else till you get to Lechlade. Tadpole is a bridge with a single span, but not an elegant one, and the river banks above here are still flat. Rushy Weir and Lock, a mile above, is a pretty bit; a fine pool, with the old broken weir and bridge nearly shut in with trees, and guarded by the Lock-house covered with foliage, the foreground crammed with river-parsley,—these make it one of the best rural scenes on the upper river. There are some nasty turns with shallows above here, and some of the gates on the towing-path are nailed up by the farmers, who have, I am informed, gone so far as to threaten proceedings against anyone trespassing (?); but I very much question if anyone dares

to stop the right of way on the towing-path However, I have traversed it several times, interrupted; and should have refused to s been asked to, as I believe I had a right to g is next passed, close to which is a small track is under a side-arch, so that, unles bridge is passed. It is a picturesque old st ornamented by a cross on the centre of its g the scene of more than one battle.

Passing upwards, we next reach Hart's W the greatest fall (about 3 ft.) of any among Thames, perhaps a word or two upon passin; not be out of place. In winter there is a but very little fall, the weir-paddles being a thing to guard against in shooting is the b rymers. I recollect one winter in passing lying on my back in the boat to get thr amount of skin off my nose and face, thro bridge whilst going under. In summer the as the bridge is a long way above the wate look out for is, the nearly direct fall of a fo ing or descending, and this perhaps in a s to get your boat through. Weirs are bui way from locks, and, to a person not usec puzzling. They take up the whole breadth in opening them fully, you let the whole of t above pass through; they are generally c ferent parts, viz. the bridge, the rymers, ar bridge is longer than the span of the stream works round on a pin; the part on the shor to balance the other, and notches cut to keep each one in its place. On the sill,

CULHAM.

CULHAM LOCK, from Abingdon Bridge, 2 miles; to Clifton Lock, 2 m. 6 fur. 130 yds.: falls from 5 feet in high to 7 ft. 6 in. in low water; average summer fall, 7 ft.

CLIFTON LOCK, from Appleford Railway Bridge, 1 m. 2 fur. 76 yds.; to Day's Lock, 2 m. 7 fur. 180 yds.: falls about 3 feet, varies but very little.

Culham Lock is reached by the cut which branches off on the left when coming down, (to the right going up). The main stream leads to Sutton Mill and pool, said to be the deepest on the river, and to harbour large fish. The last three locks together form the greatest fall, within the same distance, on the Thames. Below Culham Lock is a splendid reach for Jack and Roach, though not fished much: whilst, below Clifton Weir (on the main stream) the river abounds in Barbel and Perch.

CLIFTON.

CLIFTON BRIDGE is a neat new brick structure, spanning the river in place of the old ferry; and close below, on the top of a sharp bluff, is the very pretty church.

Inn at Clifton, "The Barley-mow," (land at the Bridge Toll-house). (See p. 60.)

Fisherman, ABRAHAM FRANKLIN.

DORCHESTER.

DAY'S LOCK, from Clifton Bridge, 2 m. 4 fur. 40 yds.; to mouth of River Thame, 6 fur. 180 yds.: falls from 1 ft. in high to 5 ft. in low water; average summer fall, about 4 feet.

The view of the river at Day's Lock, in combination with the hills in the background, forms one of those characteristic "bits"

of river scenery that our landscape-painter the hill is very fine, and the remains of round the second hill (consisting of a p to be Roman, is interesting.

Between the river and Dorchester we t low mounds (lately partly destroyed by th land), also Roman or Saxon earthworks, tant about 1 mile) is an old abbey chu Little Wittenham Church peeps through bank, and the Thame, which runs throug Thames on the left.

DAY'S LOCK. Three beds at the lock-boats taken care of or housed.

INNS.

The "White Hart."

The "Fleur-de-lis" (pronounced by the luce").

The "Crown."

Fishing.—The weirs and pools at Day' for their fine Perch, and from thence rigl is good ground for Jack, Perch, and Chul ford village is a deep hole noted for its l and there the various flams furnish a splen just where fish most abound.

FISHERMEN.

JAS. BROWN.
GEO. CHERRIL.

Bathing at the Weir.

Pic-nics at Wittenham Wood, a very fa posite the Thame Mouth.

Inn at Shillingford, the "George," up th

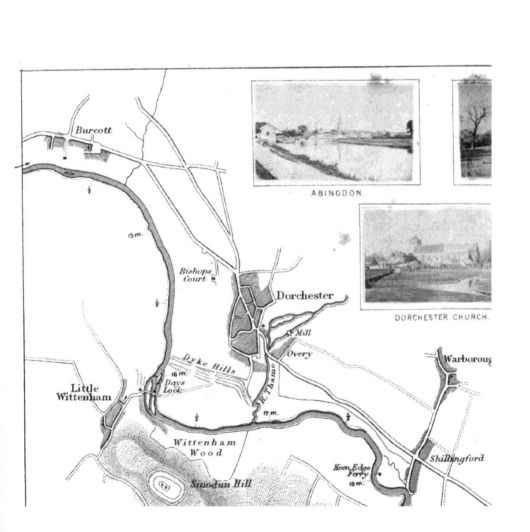

Burcott

15 m.

Bishops
Court

Dorchester

ABINGDON.

DORCHESTER CHURCH.

Mill

Overy

Dyke Hills

R. Thame

Warborough

16 m.

Days
Lock

Little
Wittenham

17 m.

Wittenham
Wood

Keen Edge
Ferry

Shillingford

Sinodun Hill

18 m.

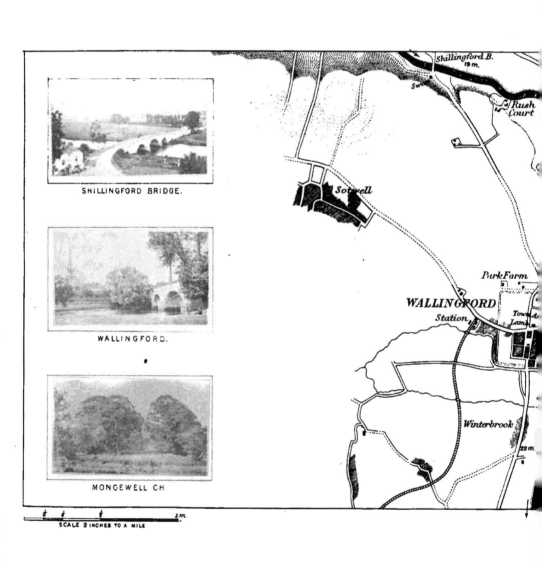

SHILLINGFORD BRIDGE.

WALLINGFORD.

MONGEWELL CH

SCALE 2 INCHES TO A MILE

Shillingford B.
19 m.

Rush
Court

Sotwell

Park Farm

WALLINGFORD

Station

Winterbrook

22 m.

SHILLINGFORD BRIDGE.

SHILLINGFORD BRIDGE, from Day's Lock, 2 m. 5 fur. 200 yds. ; to Benson Lock, 1 m. 2 fur. 30 yds.

At Shillingford Bridge the road from Oxford to Reading crosses the river, and, passing " The Swan," winds along up the hill from whence our view is taken. The walk from here along the wood-side is very pleasing, but there is no feature of note.

Hotel, the " Swan," close to the bridge. Boats housed and punts to be let. (See p. 60.)

Fishing.—Good, the water being preserved for a mile above and a mile below the bridge.

Fisherman, J. REYNOLDS, (at the " Swan").

BENSON AND EWELME.

BENSON LOCK, from Shillingford Bridge, 1 m. 2 fur. 30 yds. ; to Wallingford Bridge, 1 m. 2 fur.: falls from 3 ft. 6 in. in high to 6 ft. 6 in. in low water ; average in summer, about 5 ft. 6 in.

Benson has nothing worth visiting, its attractiveness having departed with the old coaching days that once enlivened it ; but at Ewelme, two miles off, (from Wallingford, 3½ miles by road), is a fine old church, containing a magnificent altar-tomb, richly embellished with sculptured figures, &c., to the memory of Alice, Duchess of Suffolk, the grand-daughter of the poet Chaucer ; and also the tomb of her father, Sir Thomas Chaucer, and his wife. The monumental effigy of the duchess has round its arm the Order of the Garter, being one of the very few remaining examples of this.

The Church has other interesting features, and close by are the Alms-houses built by the Duchess of Suffolk, arranged round a beautiful cloister, which of itself would amply recompense for the visit any lover of architecture.

Fisherman—WHITEMAN.

WALLINGFORI

WALLINGFORD BRIDGE, from Oxford, 21 1
Nuneham Ferry (just below Wallingford Lo

Wallingford, like Oxford, is a very ancie said, the chief city of the Attrebatii in C destroyed by the Danes in 1006, but soon and in Domesday Book is said to have co Wigod the Saxon (whose daughter married founder of Oxford Castle) built a castle her liam the Conqueror, before proceeding to battle of Hastings, received the homage of of Canterbury, and other of the chief me Empress Matilda, being pressed by Stephe fled over the snow, and was besieged by him the river by erecting a castle at Crowmarsh Wallingford Castle stood in the wars of the was one of the last places that held out fo taken and demolished by Fairfax.

There is very little now remaining. . Th terest to a stranger are, the remains of the the grounds of J. K. Hedges, Esq.), St. M Market-place, and the old earthworks (calle once enclosed the town. Crowmarsh Chui bank, is partly of Norman architecture.

HOTELS.

The " Lamb," High-street.
The " Town Arms," (close to the bridge).

INNS.

The " George."
The " Feathers."

(Continued from p. 7.)

river, exactly underneath the bridge, are corresponding sockets to hold their ends, and then the paddles fill up the spaces between each; the weight of the water above keeping all tight. Generally, for small boats, only a few of the paddles and rymers are moved, so that there is always a fall, and the best way to get up is to fasten your tow-line to the head of the boat, and gently haul her, one person being on the bridge of the weir to guide her through. As a rule, unless the weir is all out, you will not get through by any other way. Going down is different, and much easier, though somewhat dangerous (most of the weir-pools being very deep); but, having ascertained that everything is ready, pull gently on, and keep your boat's head *straight* to the centre of the opening, just before reaching which the oars must be shifted, yet kept ready to be used again the moment you are passed, as the stream rushing through causes a strong back-current. It is always better, if you have not been through before, to get help from the neighbouring cottage, refreshing yourselves, if needed; and a small quantity of the Englishman's backsheesh (beer) will always find you a willing assistant. Sometimes it is wiser, and saves time, to drag the boat over (if you can), rather than pass through; but this must be a matter for consideration at the time.

There is an Inn at Hart's Weir (no beds), and also a large pair of water-wheels, used to pump water for irrigating the land. Buscot Lock, Weir, and Brandy Distillery are next reached; but are only interesting from the extent of the works. The spirit is made from beet-root, sent to London in boats, and from thence to France, returning to us in the shape of *eau-de-vie*. Buscot village stands on the right bank, a short distance above the lock. The river for some distance pursues a serpentine course, and at last reaches St. John's Bridge and Lock, the latter lying up the small stream to the left. St. John's Lock is the first on the Thames, and is in very good repair. A little way beyond is Lechlade, looking in the distance not unlike Abingdon. Just through the

bridge is the wharf, where boats can be l⸱ the "Red Lion," will attend to your com way. The Church here is worth a visit: the Perpendicular style, with a beautiful ⸱ inside requires a few of its embellishme⸱ a good view of it from the river.

A short mile beyond Lechlade the n ceases; and, passing through a lock at I⸱ it enters the Thames and Severn Canal, wl the Thames as far as Cricklade, and then ⸱ Head. In the winter, and very early spr⸱ up the river to Water Hay Bridge, but i⸱ practicable. Years ago the navigation and perhaps to Water Hay Bridge; but o⸱ canal, the river-trade was transferred, and tl fairly grown up; so much so, that in ge some time ago, I walked nearly three mile⸱ river's bed, dragging at the head of my ⸱ thing but agreeable. Of the weirs, Ingles⸱ existence, having been dragged out by th⸱ Ham Weir, about 3 miles above, and Ke⸱ above, only the sills remain; they being stones on, to cross the river. I can fi⸱ weirs still higher; one at Cricklade—ra⸱ trace,—and one about $2\frac{1}{2}$ miles above t⸱ sheeting of which are still in fair order, in ⸱

Of things worth notice above Lechlad⸱ Inglesham Church (Early English), a little picturesque belfry, and having a curiousl⸱ one of its walls; Kempsford Church, $5\frac{1}{2}$ ⸱ men of fourteenth-century work, with a ⸱ of the dukes of Lancaster; Castle Eato⸱ $1\frac{1}{2}$ mile further on—both picturesque; ⸱

miles by the river from Lechlade, with its two Churches; one simple and quiet, and the other with a splendid tower. There are also two crosses in fair preservation here, which stand in the churchyards. The "White Horse," close to the upper church, is the Inn to stop at; and your boat, if you go up the river, will be taken care of at the first cottage you come to (Rose Cottage), just after passing under a unique plank-bridge; but, if you are on the canal, at the wharf. The nearest Railway Station to Cricklade is at Purton, 3½ miles off; but if you take a boat down by rail, go to Minety, the next station as you may better meet with a conveyance th

In conclusion I would add, that I shall be further detail that may be required by any visiting Oxford, *en route* for the upper Than surveyed and photographed the greater part Thames Head, and have traversed it sevel seasons of the year.

DISTANCES TO INGLESHAM.

(Some of these are estimated, others measured.)

Oxford Bridge to						m. fur. yds.	Oxford Bridge to				
Medley Weir	.	.	.	.	.	2 0 11	New Bridge	.	.	.	.
Godstow Lock	.	.	.	.	.	3 3 45	Tadpole Bridge	.	.	.	.
Eynsham Weir	.	.	.	.	.	7 4 135	Radcot Bridge	.	.	.	.
Pinkle Lock	.	.	.	.	.	9 3 33	Hart's Weir	.	.	.	.
Skinner's Weir	.	.	.	.	.	10 3 33	Buscot Lock	.	.	.	.
Bablock Hythe Ferry	.	.	.	.	12 0 86	St. John's Bridge .	.	.	.	.
(This place is only 4¾ miles from Oxford, through Cumnor.)							Lechlade Bridge .	.	.	.	.
Ridge's Weir	.	.	.	.	.	15 1 0	Inglesham Round-house	.	.	.	.

TOLLS FOR PLEASURE-BOATS, (GIGS, &c.,) ON THE THAMES AND SEVERN

Lechlade (Inglesham) to Cricklade, 10s.; ditto to Thames Head, or any place on the summit level, 20s.; ditto to S understanding, in respect to the last two items, that the boats are lifted over (with the Lock-keeper's assistance) at so the summit level, whenever this is required.

WALLINGFORD (continued).

Boats housed and to be let.

J. CLOWDESLEY.

THOS. RANSOM ("Town Arms"), both close above the bridge.

WALLINGFORD RAILWAY STATION (Branch line, G.W.R.), in the Wantage-road.

Fishing.—The fishing above Wallingford Bridge was very poor; but since the new bye-laws of the Conservancy have come into operation it is improving. Below Wallingford Bridge, on the right bank, is the influx of a most disgraceful open sewer, with water (?) thoroughly black and thick; an ugly prospect in case of an epidemic; and from here to the lock are coarse fish in numbers, but of small size.

The river below the lock ought to be excellent, but it does not bear a good name.

FISHERMEN.

JOHN CLOWDESLEY.
JOSEPH GUNSTONE.

WALLINGFORD LOCK is open in high water, and does not fall at any time above 18 inches. It is, I am informed, decided to remove it at an early date.

H. W. TAUNT'S Agent at Wallingford: Mr. PAYNE, Stationer, Market-place.

MOULSFORI

MOULSFORD FERRY, from Wallingford, 3 Cleeve Lock, 1 m. 2 fur. 78 yds.

MOULSFORD STATION (G.W.R.), distant ?

The scenery by the river from Walling what flat: the only object of interest bein; park and residence not far below Walling overhanging the water help to break the scape, whilst the Church, peeping between fine itself, yet makes a pretty view. The vil retained the same name ever since the D it belonged to Roger de Laci, and was wor

Before Moulsford is reached, the river under the line of the G.W.R.: just above group of aits, is a good spot for Jack, Per right bank stands Moulsford Church; from a favourite sailing reach, abounding in fish.

Inn at Moulsford Ferry, the "Beetle and are to be let. (See p. 61.)

FISHERMEN.

F. STRANGE (Bow Bridge); WM. COX; ?
Bathing just above the Ferry.

CLEVE.—*Overfall at*

CLEVE REACH.

STREATLEY.

Common
Cholsey
G.W.R.
Asylu
Moulsford Station
24 m.
Moulsford
25 m.
Ferry
Beetle & Wedge

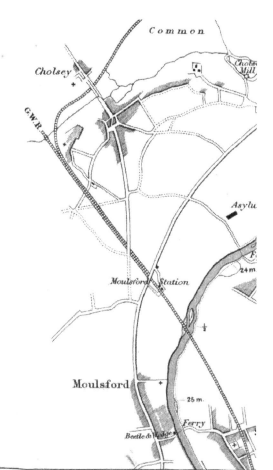

Streatley Farm
The Spring
Spring Farm
26 m.
Cleeve Lock
Cleeve
27 m.
Streatley
Lock
Miller of Mansfield
Bull
Station
Goring
Common Wood
28 m.
The Grotto
Ferry
29 m.

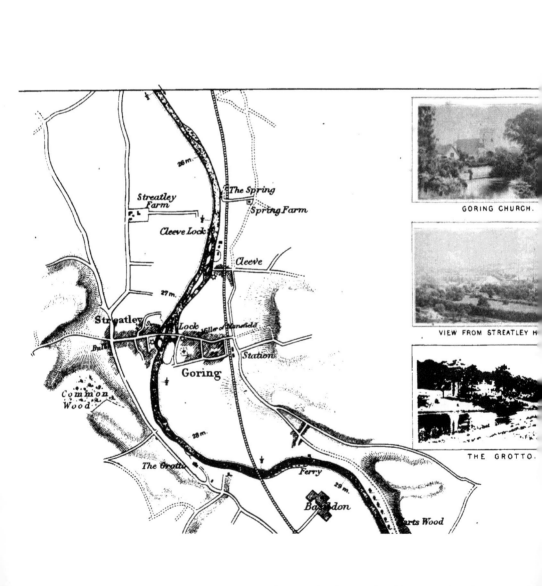

GORING CHURCH.

VIEW FROM STREATLEY H

THE GROTTO.

CLEEVE.

THE "Leather Bottle" Inn (no beds), on the left bank, 3 fur. above the Lock. Here is a well-known spring, the waters of which are said to act as a cure for sprains, &c.

CLEEVE LOCK, from Moulsford Ferry, 1 m. 2 fur. 78 yds.; to Goring Lock, 5 fur. (the shortest distance between locks on the river, that between Hurley and Temple Locks being 5 fur. 23 yds.): falls from 3 ft. 6 in. in high to 5 ft. in low water; average in summer, about 4 ft. 6 in.

There are about Cleeve some sweet spots, that well repay notice. The old mill from Goring-field; and, facing the other way, distant Streatley with its splendid background of hills, the river at their feet reflecting in its mirror each inverted object; the old weir, with its broken campsheding; and between the islands, the overfall spanned by its bridge of simple rustic style:—these cannot but charm and enchain the eye.

GORING AND STREATLEY.

GORING LOCK, from Cleeve Lock, 5 fur.; to Gate-Hampton Ferry, 1 m. 4 fur. 127 yds.: falls from 3 ft. 6 in. in high to 4 ft. 6 in. in low water; average in summer, about 4 feet.

STATION AT GORING (G.W.R. main line), about half-a-mile from the bridge.

The twin villages of Goring and Streatley are separated by the river, which expands to some width, and contains several islands. The two places are connected by a picturesque wooden toll-bridge. Goring is on the left bank, and close to the mill stands the Church, an object of interest, the finest view of which is to be had from the bridge. Originally it consisted of only one lofty Norman aisle and tower without a chancel, but a north aisle was afterwards added, and at subsequent periods, porches and other projections were stuck on.

Streatley, on the opposite bank of the river, is well known, from the beautiful and extensive views to be obtained from its lovely hills. The view for miles, both up a of that soft, flowing character, which is ess the Thames, winding along from the botto extreme distance, gives life and motion to a Streatley is said to owe its name to Icknie entered Berkshire by a ford through the riv lately been restored.

At Aldworth, nearly three miles from her a Norman Church, the interior of which c curious monumental effigies in stone, repr the family of De la Beche, who built a c buried in the Church. These figures, nine injury during the civil wars at the hands of but are still in tolerably good preservation.

INNS AT STREATL:

The "Swan," near the river. (See p. 61.)
The "Bull," up the village. (See p. 61.)

INNS AT GORINC

The "Miller of Mansfield."
The "Sloane Arms" (close to the Station

Boats to be let and hous

*SAM SAUNDERS (at the "Swan," Streatle:

Fishing.—The fishing at Streatley and good: the waters being preserved for a pools splendid Chub and other fish abour river to Cleeve is excellent water, affor Below, Pike and Perch are everywhere to to Hart's Wood.

FISHERMEN.

J. SAUNDERS; E. MILES; J. RUSH.

Fish.—Pike, Chub, Perch, Dace, Roach,

Bathing on the Goring side, about 200 y:

H. W. TAUNT'S Agent at Streatley: Mr. G(

SCENE ON THE THAMES, SOMEWHERE BETWEEN LECHLADE AND L(

Time, May, 1872.—*Punt and Tackle in waiting.*

A SKETCH, BY GREVILLE F.

"WELL, Ben," from the angler.

"Well, Sir," from Ben.

"All ready, Ben? the train is somewhat late, so let's to work."

"No use yet, Sir. There's full an hour yet to spare before the fish 'll be on the feed, and it 'll take me all that to go up to the village and get the lunch on board."

"Yes, Ben, you're right! I forgot all about *our* bait. Let's have some cold meat and cheese, and if you can, a nice crusty loaf, and say—how much beer?"

"Well, as usual I suppose, Sir."

"Good, I'll leave that to you."

"And a little drop of gin, Sir?"

"Yes, yes, Ben, get what you like. But look sharp, as I want to get afloat, whether the fish are waiting for us or not."

Ben, in about an hour, is seen coming down the village to-wards the water with an earthenware bottle in one hand and the other assisting a lad to carry a heavy basket, or rather hamper. All on board, angler and man, shove off. Angler puts his tackle together, and declaring his intention to spin for a trout, asks Ben to give him a nice little bleak or dace out of the well. Ben goes on punting up stream and close into the bank under the willows, the branches of which every now and then jeopardise the angler's wide-awake, but Ben is both dumb and deaf. Ben is asked again for a bait.

"Bait!" echoes Ben, sarcastically, "bait, where am I to get bait? I marn't have no net worth a cuss, and it would take me a day with such as I have to get a dozen fit for a flight of hooks.

If I throw away a day, who's to pay me a-piece wouldn't do it, nor tuppence, nor tl

"Well, Ben, the new regulations are cer fisherman and angler; but I thought you a proper net, and no notice would be taker

"A few!" cried Ben, contemptuously, " Bailie is in a good humour, fifty, or maybe 'a few;' but if he's sulky, or I arn't not g why half-a-dozen's a few, or a few is onl I arn't going to risk a summons. I've had a rye-peck in, and lost the customer who I won't show up, as he knows I shall ask hin it be law, and I'll do it—or if it arn't law, v both the risk and the fish."

"Well, Ben, that's but fair, anyhow. I I must put up my spinning-tackle again; a a good swim, we'll try for a bait or two, stand the chance of having a lark with a ba legally kill a trout."

"All right, Sir, that's talking sensible. a better spot, and while I fixes the punt yo of pudding or two to bring 'um round."

"Igh, igh, Ben!" And the angler tuc paratory to diving into the ground-bait t and clay, but looks around in vain for that

"Where's the ground-bait, Ben?"

"Why, arn't you got none? You said

bait in your letter, and some of my customers are so precious particular that they say country bread won't do,—the bran we get from the mill is either too coarse or too pollardy, and even the clay beant stiff enough, or is too stiff and holds the stuff too long, so they all'is now brings their own dumplings."

"Well, Ben, that's a pretty go! I have not brought any; but we can throw in a few gentles or worms in the Nottingham style. I have always been of opinion that we use too much ground-bait, rather satiating the fish than creating an appetite amongst them, so I'll begin to strike an average and go without ground-bait for once."

"That's right, Sir; you're what our clergyman who fishes with me calls a feeling hofficer."

"A philosopher, I suppose you mean, Ben, but you are complimentary. It is only because I can't help it I submit; so give us your gentle-box."

"Here it is, Sir."

"Why, Ben, this is empty."

"I knows it is, and I thought you axed for it to fill it. You don't mean to say you've not brought no gentles, when you was amongst tons of 'um in London; and we arn't allowed to breed 'um now, 'cos of the Sanitary 'spector."

"No bait, no ground-bait, no gentles, Ben! well, this is a sell. Perhaps you havn't any worms?"

"You're right there, Sir; who would expect worms arter April? Why, they've gone down into the middle of the earth for moisture, and you might dig your heart out before you saw the tail of one."

A dead silence on the part of fisherman and angler for five minutes; the feelings of each must be guessed at. The former's eye is upon the stone bottle, the latter's steadily fixed on the bottom of the punt. The angler is the first to break silence.

"Ben."

"Yes, Sir."

"What are we to do?"

"Let's have summut to drink."

This is too much for the good-humoured a out into a hearty roar of laughter, which I affirmative, and the bung flies upwards from accordingly. A good swig and Ben's week's his sleeve; Ben appears a little more geni serving, "Well, this is a go! who'd a though you, who have been at it from a babe, would out nuffen you wanted. I could forgive a Co gone out afore, but it's unnatural to the likes precious bitter, Sir; I'll just take a thumb a crust of bread."

"Cold pork did you say, Ben? Is it boil Eureka! we are saved, we are saved!"

"What's up now, Sir?"

"Here, Ben, don't throw that rind away. sharp knife will do the business. There, se spectacles could tell those choice bits from have some roach yet, Ben. See, I throw bread, and if they won't take the pork we withal to make some paste. We shall do I've got a roach, and a bouncer; he cannot quarters of a pound. Where there is one, tl Another, by George! and now—no, I misse great an eagerness—I have him though. Ben, fish are not of the Jewish persuasion."

"No, Sir, the perswasion appears to l chuckled at his joke. "But in all my days I ever knowed roach to take pork."

"There is nothing new in it, Ben; it is a in the absence of gentles. Why, I knew a ﹛

PANGBOURNE AND WHITCHURCH.

WHITCHURCH LOCK, from Basildon Ferry, 2 m. 4 fur. 33 yds.; to Mapledurham Lock, 2 m. 2 fur. 70 yds.: falls from 3 ft. in high to 4 ft. 6 in. in low water; average in summer, about 4 feet.

STATION AT PANGBOURNE (G.W.R. main line), not far from the river.

"Pangbourne is another of those pearls of English landscape which our river threads, no sweeter spot is within many miles. The Thames seems especially fond of disporting itself here, and loth indeed to leave, it loiters in the great depth of the pools, creeps slily under the banks, frolics as a kitten after its tail in the eddies, and then dashes hurriedly off beneath the far-stretching pretty wooden bridge, as if to make up for time truantly lost." This is the description of the scenery at Pangbourne by Greville Fennell, one of our best Thames Anglers (in his book "The Rail and the Rod;" a work of which I can only say,— if you have not got it—get it at once): and I need add but little. The views from Shooter's Hill well repay the toil of climbing; being another edition (quite as handsomely bound) of the beautiful Streatley views. The Church and Mill of Whitchurch, viewed from the bridge, make a pretty group.

HOTELS AT PANGBOURNE.

The "Elephant and Castle." (See p. 61.)
The "George."

INNS.

The "Swan" (close to the Weir).
The "Cross Keys."

HOTEL AT WHITCHURCH.

The "Bridge House."

Boats to be let or housed.

T. ASHLEY (at the "Swan," Pangbourne).

Fishing.—The fishing at Pangbourne is noted for its fine Trout, and is well preserved by Mr. Ford, the obliging landlord of the "Elephant and Castle" (who rents the wa Lodge boat-house to Hardwicke); it is al roughly depended upon.

The pool is a noted spot, and is 25 f 150 Trout have been taken out of this | Greville Fennell, and I can well believe hi is private property.

FISHERMEN.

JOHN CHAMP.
THOS. LOVEGROVE.
WILLIAM DAVIDSON.

Fish.—Trout, Perch, Barbel, Chub, Ro; Bathing in the Weir-pool.

MAPLEDURH

MAPLEDURHAM LOCK, from Whitchurc to the "Roebuck," 7 fur. 145 yds.: falls 7 ft. in low water.; average in summer, ab

About Mapledurham is one of the mc Thames. A short distance above the Lc Hardwicke House, a fine specimen of a to have been the hiding-place, for a tim from the opposite side of the river, with th it looks very striking, and it will also rep; The view of the old Mill at Mapledurham on the river), with the combination of th its roof, and embosomed in foliage, forms (scenes that it is possible to imagine, and i its beauty and harmony. The Manor-ho also a splendid specimen of the Elizabeth are few in any part of England that are fin tion. It has always belonged to the famil still in their possession. From the front tends a broad avenue of elm trees, about a a magnificent setting to a noble picture.

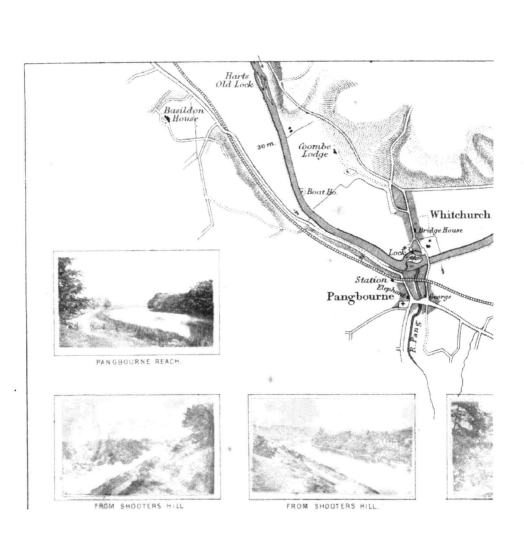

Harts
Old Lock

Basildon
House

30 m.

Coombe
Lodge

Boat Ho.

Whitchurch

Bridge House

Lock

Station

Elephant

Pangbourne

George

R. Pang

PANGBOURNE REACH.

FROM SHOOTERS HILL

FROM SHOOTERS HILL.

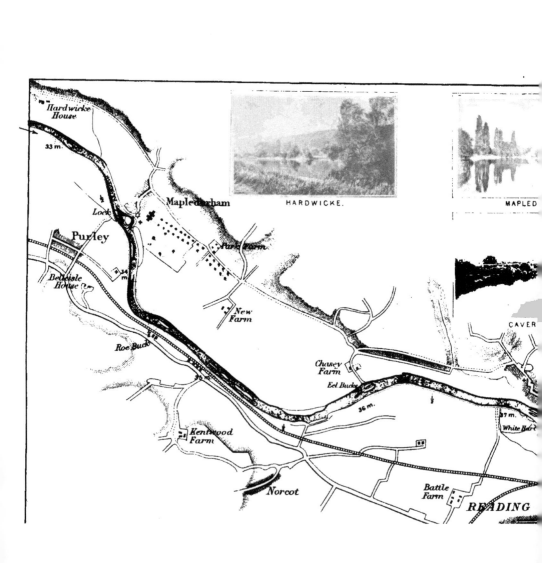

HARDWICKE.

MAPLED

CAVER

Hardwicke
House

33 m.

Lock

Mapledurham

Purley

Park Farm

Bellisle
House

34
m.

New
Farm

Roe Buck

Chazey
Farm

Eel Bucks

36 m.

37 m.

White Hart

Kentwood
Farm

Norcot

Battle
Farm

READING

The Lock also, in combination with the Weir, is well worth notice, presenting at every turn a varied arrangement, each variation as lovely as the last. Mapledurham is essentially a " Painter's Paradise." A short mile below we reach the " Roebuck" Inn, fantastically perched on the side of the railway embankment ; and looking back, Purley House shews itself amongst the trees.

From thence to Caversham the river-view is flat and uninteresting, after the splendid scenes we have left behind ; but it improves as we near that village, where the Church with its wooden tower, mounted partly up a hill rising from the river, is a picturesque object.

No Inns at Mapledurham.

The " Roebuck" Inn, on the right bank, 7 fur. 145 yds. below the Lock.

Fishing.—The fishing here is rented by Thos. Lovegrove, of Pangbourne, and has vastly improved since it has been in his possession. It is known for its large Trout, Jack, Chub, and Perch. As the preservation of the water begins where the previous section of the Pangbourne water ends, we are quite safe in saying that the whole is preserved, from above " Coombe House" to the " Roebuck," a distance of some 4 miles.

From thence to Caversham the fishing is still good, but not so fine as that last spoken of, in consequence of its having been severely netted ; but I hardly think it deserves the bad name it seems to have acquired amongst the fishermen of the river.

FISHERMEN.

THOS. LOVEGROVE, (Pangbourne).
EDWARD SHEPHEARD, at the Lock-house.

CAVERSHAM and READING.

CAVERSHAM BRIDGE, from Mapledurham Lock, 3 m. 6 fur. 131 yds. ; to Caversham Lock, 4 fur. 120 yds.

CAVERSHAM LOCK, from Oxford, 37 m. 7 fur. 170 yds. ; to

Sonning Lock, 2 m. 4. fur. 148 yds. : falls 4 ft. in low water ; average in summer, abou

READING. Stations at about 5 furlon Bridge.

G. W. R. main line.

S. W. R., Reading Branch, }
S. E. R.,   ,,   ,, } run into the

The G. W. R. Station at Reading is div parts, but plans are in preparation for the c Station, when it will become an ordinary dou the inconvenience that arises from its being removed. At present, the up Station is the the entrance from Friars-street, and the ol the down Station.

Reading, the capital of Berks, is situated the River on the right bank. It is a gro manufacturing town. Its chief objects of i ruins, situated in the Forbury Gardens ; Lawrence and St. Mary, in the Butts ; and Messrs. Huntley and Palmer. The Ab Henry I., and endowed by him in the n On his death, which happened at Rouen, hi wrapt in bull-hides, brought here and bur The Abbey was dissolved in the reign of I and the abbot, Hugh Faringdon, and two and quartered, for denying the king's suprei

Reading was besieged in 1643 by the P Essex, and surrendered a few days after ; t fortified were blown up by them on the ten The Abbey suffered greatly during this ti garded until lately as a quarry, large masses to repair and enlarge the parish churches, a the bridge on the Wargrave-road, at Park by the late General Conway. It is now v

(Continued from p. 15.)

Broads who were as badly off for bait as we are, taking a large basket of roach with roast goose. Here, I've got a pretty bleak at last. There, I will put my float shallower. Yes, I am now amongst the fry, and have enough to commence spinning, so up poles and go to work, Ben."

Ben shakes his ears slightly at the word "work," but to do him justice commences punting with sufficient judgment to give ample opportunities for the angler to display his skill in spinning, and presently elicits several ejaculations of "well cast," "beautiful," and "that ought to have 'um if anything did," from Ben; but after three or four small jack and a perch or two were successfully caught and thrown back again, as being too small for capture, and a goodly trout was hooked, Ben became perfectly enthusiastic, and looked on at the excellent play with unfeigned admiration, finally lifting the exhausted fish into the punt for his customer with a whoop of delight that made the neighbouring woods echo again. It was fully eight pounds in weight, and in splendid condition, the largest and finest, as Ben declared, that had been killed that season. It certainly was a most beautiful fish, and deserved the praise bestowed upon it. Another bleak was soon on the flight with the prettiest possible bend, to make it spin true and well, and our angler is about to commence again, when his arm is arrested by Ben.

"What, Sir!" he exclaims.

"What's the matter, Ben ¿

"What's the matter!" exclaims Ben, in apparent astonishment at the question, "What's the matter! why, we arn't wetted it."

This is a custom which is greatly honoured on the Thames upon the taking of a more than usually good fish, and is seldom or never dispensed with, if the necessary offerings of liquor are at hand to do full justice to the ceremony. It is, indeed, stoutly maintained by the Thames fishermen that this sacrifice upon the Altar of Luck is necessary to propitiate the river-god, without which exhibition of spirit upon the part of the fisherman, the

aquatic deity invariably refuses to assist b᷎ the fish. Whether this be so or not, it wa᷎ that the taste of the gin was scarcely out he was called upon again to lift another tr᷎ of not more than half the size of the forme᷎

"Cuss that gin!" exclaimed Ben, after lo shortcomings of the second fish. "Cuss th᷎ enough to put more pounds on. Do you I should bring in over that ere gin if I ᷎ should have it, 'Found drowned.'"

"Perhaps double the quantity would ma᷎ Ben," suggests the angler.

"That's it, Sir; I ought a' thought of ᷎ made up for any neglect in the particul᷎ ever, truth compels us to state that alth᷎ appealed to very often and most devout juniper-berry appeared to have departed, could Ben induce, with all his pulling at t᷎ to immolate itself on the barbarous tri᷎ tackle.

"But what are you dodging behind my ᷎ have me in the river."

"Why, Sir, don't yer see them foot-hogg᷎

"Yes; they are photographers, Ben. I staff of assistants. They'll have you and thing."

"Not if I knows on it," cries Ben, ducki᷎ to side like a toy-mandarin; "tho' they d᷎ a fellow with a bull's eye as quick as a fla᷎ a holiday. They got my missus on'st whil᷎ my guernsey to dry, and made a lady on h᷎ thousands and thousands on, at a shilling woman has never bin herself since. Such come up! But there now!" exclaimed Be᷎ who had dropped a gold watch overboard, "while I bin talking to you, Sir, I'm blamed if I don't believe they've got me, for I felt for a moment just as if I had bin picked up and dabbed as flat as a pancake on a plate, and stuck in a windy for ever. I don't call such proceedings as them all taut* and above-board ;" and Ben supplemented a grin at his own joke.

Could Ben, however, have been mesmerised as well as photographed? We must leave this philosophical question for the Oxford professors.

And now the clouds collect, the atmosphere gets chilly, Ben has contrived to drink up all the beer, and the angler considers it is time to prepare for his return by train.

"I pity those who has given away their winter togs," remarks Ben, with a dash of Christian sympathy, as he shoved towards the landing.

"Yes, Ben; but they must have warm hearts, Ben."

"Ah, I didn't think of that, Sir, God bless 'um! It's never been my chance though to find one of that sort," added Ben, looking down at his own rusty velveteen.

* Ben mistook my name, but I don't TAUNT him about it.—ED.

"That's well thought of, Ben; you hav(mine, and a shooting-coat, and some tackle

"Yes, Sir."

"Well, you may keep those, Ben; I dar the colder for it. This is indeed an inc extra thick coat is needed on the water botl

"God bless yer, Sir! You're the right so time I gets a letter from you, there sharn't l worms, nor gentles, sharn't there? if I has t a well for 'um, and ten mile for the clay. Thank'e, Sir; that sov. 'll make it right wit public; and here's your trout, Sir, done up missus, who sends her respects. I throw again, cos it's close time—and here's the tra And so say we, "Good afternoon, Ben," bu either that the angler should never leave th(of bait to the fisherman, or give such instru his providing so necessary a requirement, a shewn that even where the general char(absent, with a little tact sport is not altog(of the ingenious angler.

as a pleasure garden and promenade, and the huge remaining masses of cemented flint and rubble still give a faint idea of its former greatness. The old gateway has been carefully restored, and is used as an armoury for the volunteers. St. Lawrence's Church stands at the top of the Market-place, and St. Mary's in the centre of the town. The Biscuit Factory, which employs some 700 hands, can be visited by order obtained on application.

Inn at Caversham, the " White Hart," on the bridge.

HOTELS, (Reading).

The " Queen's," Friars-street.
The " George," King-street.
The " Great Western," close to the Stations.
The " Duke of Edinburgh," Caversham-road.
The " Bee-hive" Commercial Coffee-house, Friars-street.

Boats to be let and housed, (Caversham).

J. R. PIPER, Caversham Bridge. (See p. 62.)
E. CAUSTON (see p. 62), K. FREEBODY, W. WAIGHT, C. BEST, Caversham.
F. KNIGHT, Caversham Lock.

FISHERMEN.

W. MOSS, (Piper's, Caversham Bridge); P. FREEBODY; H. KNIGHT.

Bathing at the Reading Bathing-house, near the Lock.

KENNETT'S MOUTH. From Caversham Lock, 4 fur. 120 yds.; to Sonning Lock, 1 m. 7 fur. 28 yds. The river Kennett joins here, running from Newbury, where it meets the Kennett and Avon Canal, by which the West of England, &c., may be reached by water, (see also under Abingdon, ante).

Boats to let.

J. HOLMES, at the Ferry, (also a house-boat).
J. P. HALL, on Kennett.
—. FOX, " Dreadnought" Inn.
Inn, the " Dreadnought."
Fisherman, J. P. HALL.

H. W. TAUNT'S Agents at Reading: Mr. LOVEJOY, Library, London-street, (see p. 62); Mr. BRAGG, Stationer, Broad-street.

SONNING

SONNING LOCK, from Caversham Lock, to Shiplake Lock, 2 m. 6 fur. 126 yds.: ? to 5 ft. in low water; average in summer, a Twyford Station (G. W. R.), from Sonni

The River after leaving Caversham runs meadows, one of which is the Reading r just before reaching Sonning it turns sh woods of Holme Park, along the edge of walk, the trees overhanging the towing-pat At Sonning the river branches out, encircli and passing the Lock, where a glance at Sa repaid by the insight gained into their ? the bridge. On the right bank stands the (seeing : in the interior is a unique arch a with sculptured figures, representing on (the twelve Apostles, and opposite the ? other figures. There is also a curious monuments. Sadler at the Lock keeps the

Boats to be let and hou

J. SADLER, at the Lock. (See p. 62.)

HOTELS.

The "White Hart," close to the bridge ; ? the side stream, under the towing-path brid
Inn, The " Butchers' Arms," up the villa
Fishing.—The fishing at Sonning is ve pools are the private property of Mr. ? of the back water is rented by W. Hull, a Permission to fish is freely given by Mr. when previously engaged).

FISHERMEN.

JAS. BROMLEY ; WM. HULL, " French H
Fish.—Trout, Barbel, Chub, Jack, ? Gudgeon, &c.

Bathing at the Weir, by permission of ? in the stream near the " French Horn."

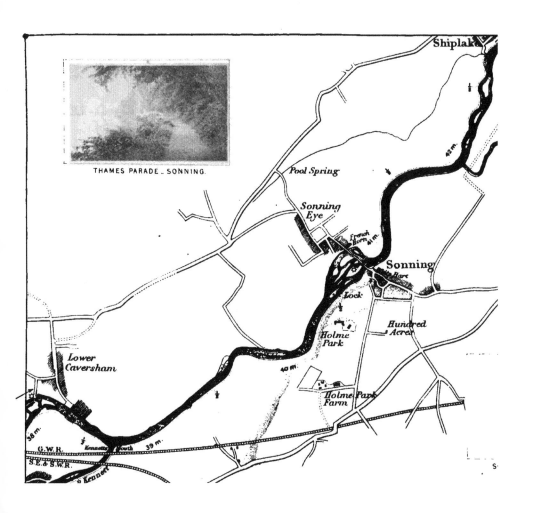

THAMES PARADE - SONNING.

Shiplake

Pool Spring

Sonning
Eye

French
Horn 41 m.

Sonning

Bart

Lock

Hundred
Acres

Holme
Park

Lower
Caversham

40 m.

Holme Park
Farm

38 m.

G.W.R.   Kennetts Mouth   39 m.

S.E. & S.W.R.

Kennett

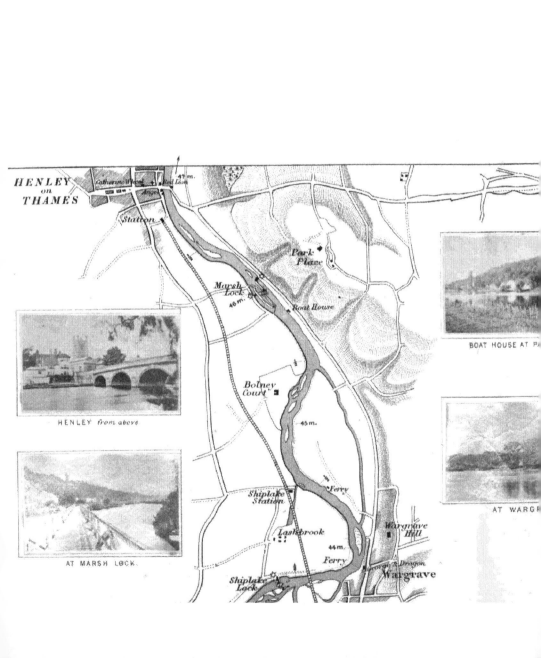

HENLEY
on
THAMES

Station

Marsh
Lock
46 m.

Boat House

Park
Place

47 m.

Bolney
Court

45 m.

Shiplake
Station

Lashbrook

44 m.

Ferry

Ferry

Shiplake
Lock

Wargrave
Hill

Ferry

Wargrave

HENLEY from above

AT MARSH LOCK.

BOAT HOUSE AT PA

AT WARGR

WARGRAVE.

SHIPLAKE LOCK, from Sonning Bridge, 2 m. 4 fur. 66 yds.; to Shiplake Ferry, 1 m. 0 fur. 38 yds.: falls from 1 ft. 6 in. in high to 4 ft. in low water; average in summer, 3 ft. 6 in.

SHIPLAKE STATION (G.W.R., Henley Branch), from Wargrave Ferry, about 6 fur.

After leaving Sonning, we pass nothing noticeable till nearing Shiplake, where the Church, mounted on a hill close above a large chalk-pit, is an interesting feature. Dr. Phillmore Island also, with a peep at Shiplake Mill beyond, must not be left unobserved, and then Wargrave comes into view. Just below Shiplake Lock the Loddon joins the Thames; this stream is celebrated by being the subject of the fabled story of "Lodona" in Pope's "Windsor Forest."

Wargrave was once a market-town; but from its greatness it has dwindled down into a pleasant village. The Church (the tower of which is beautifully overgrown with ivy) stands close to a backwater running up from the main stream; but to visit it, a detour through the village is necessary. It contains a monumental tablet to the memory of Mr. Day (author of "Sandford and Merton"), who was killed here by a fall from his horse. Below Wargrave our attention is arrested by the beautiful background of hills, with the mansions embosomed among their clothing of woods; and nearing Marsh Lock, the river runs along at the foot of some bold cliffs, forming part of the grounds of Park Place. These pleasure-grounds are ornamented by a very picturesque boat-house in the Gothic style, which, with the bridge built from the walls of Reading Abbey, must not be passed by; there is also, among other objects of interest, the Druids' Temple, presented by the inhabitants of Jersey to General Conway. Permission to view the grounds of Park Place can generally be obtained, by sending a request previously.

Hotel, the "George and Dragon" ("Ferry Hotel").

INNS.

The "White Hart."
The "Bull."

Boats housed and to le
W. WYATT, at Wargrave Ferry.

Fishing.—The fishing below Sonning to S class character. Greville Fennell says, "Ship its Pike; but holds few Trout. Now we get Island, at the tail of which there are ple spectable girth, and Jack in due season. the fly may be profitably cast for Chub an House is on the hill, and about 400 yard known Chalk-pit Hole, and the angler can place, making an exception here and there ning. I heard of seventy brace of Perch with two rods at the Chalk-pit in a day caught Perch there for a short time tha number."

Below Shiplake to Marsh Lock, Roach, abound; and in some of the backwaters a Pool is known for Barbel, and below are fi affording good fishing right down to Henle

FISHERMEN.
R. WYATT; F. WYATT; —. TOWNSEND.

Fish.—Jack, Chub, Perch, Tench, Roach

Bathing at the Lock-pool; also behind t Wargrave.

MARSH LOCK, from Shiplake Ferry, 2 Henley Bridge, 7 fur. 109 yds.: falls from 2 in low water; average in summer, about 4 f

CAMPING OUT, No. 1.—(IN A TENT.)

By R. W. S.

THE picturesque and varying scenery about the river, combined with excellent sport both with gun and rod, can under no circumstances be more thoroughly enjoyed and with such advantage as under canvas, or what is now generally known as "Camping out." It would be useless to dilate upon the manifold, indeed always new, beauties that are constantly to be found on or about the banks; but in giving a slight *résumé* of the necessary precautions to be observed in camping, one cannot adopt a better course than to follow the movements of the "Rovers," who claim, under the guidance of Captain South, precedence in the amateur camping world. The experience of many years has enabled that gentleman to furnish us with accurate information, which may perhaps prove acceptable to our readers.

1. In selecting a tent, care should be taken to avoid all unnecessary pegs, guy-lines, and poles; these not only prove cumbersome in travelling, but are, ofttimes, utterly useless. The "Rovers'" tent, made by Paget and Sons, Aldersgate-street, E.C., is recommended as being for practical purposes the most useful. It gives an area of 10 ft. by 9, a height of 6 ft., has only two pegs, and can be fixed and ready for occupation in three minutes. These advantages, combined with simplicity and lightness (the whole weighing under 28 lbs.), are difficult to be surpassed.

2. Especial attention should be directed to the selection of a suitable piece of land (that on a very slight incline is preferable), but above all the exclusion of damp, the forerunner of acute rheumatism, should be carefully studied; a most terrible result may arise if this be not carefully attended to, and although the land at the time of pitching the tent may be comparatively baked by a burning sun, yet ere morning a dam[p] river will rise, that on many occasions has incautious campers. The mere covering quite insufficient, and the most effective is "Croggon's Roofing Asphalte;" this, al bulk, is very light, and forms, when laid able substitute for a mattress, and is thor has been found that the ordinary macintos bulk, is not so well suited for the purpose.

It is to be regretted that the habit grounds, without previously obtaining perm thereof, has of late been on the increase. more especially between Maidenhead and the most lovely parts of river scenery can such permission is not requisite.

Proceeding: after erecting the tent, cov and using one's decorative powers in the may next be called to the culinary arrange

3. The variety of cooking apparatus gives a large field for selection, but the mo are, in all cases, desirable. A camping more than three good meals per diem, luncheon, 1 P.M.; dinner at 6 P.M. Each easily cooked by even an inexperienced pe of a small book published by the well-kno and Co., entitled "Plain Cookery," they of an epicure. The advantages possesse compense any reader who may invest th

Penny in its purchase, for it not only gives the quantities required for various numbers, but also the average cost of each article. Several inventions have of late years been introduced in the list of domestic necessaries, and for camping purposes; some prove of the greatest value. We mention a few, for the guidance of intending explorers :—Swiss milk, in tins; essence of coffee, cocoa and milk, in tins; preserved meats; potted meats, fish, soups, &c.

The next important item to receive attention should be a store-box, and we are enabled to give a list of the contents of the " Rovers'" box, which measures 3 ft. + 18 in. + 12 in. ; it is duly partitioned off, and all available space made to serve some purpose. Contents :—6 knives, 6 forks ; 1 carving ditto ; 1 cooking ditto ; 12 spoons ; 1 sardine-knife ; 12 plates, 3 dishes ; 1 flour-box ; 1 sugar-box (loaf) ; 1 ditto (moist) ; 1 salt-jar ; 1 tea-can (1 lb.) ;

1 coffee ditto (1 lb.) ; tea-pot, 6 cups an(
pepper-pot ; salt-cellar ; mustard-pot ; herb-t;
anchovy ditto ; ketchup ; milk-tin ; cocoa-
chest, &c. A portion is also left for the
jams, or marmalade, and dry stores. Fresh
procurable at nearly all the villages *en route,*
kept separate from other stores.

In conclusion, we wish to recommend to readers the necessity of a plentiful supply covering, as, although the heat in the int(variably oppressive during the day and ev sphere changes greatly in the early morning, covering, the occupants would possibly recei be productive of evil results.

A WEEK DOWN THE THAMES.

To those who can only spare a week on our favourite river, the following hints will be useful. Arrange with Salters, or George West, of Oxford, (see pp. 56 and 58), for a boat, stating number of party, and kind of boat required ; then by rail to Oxford, spend a day there, not forgetting to give Taunt a call, and inspect his Views of Oxford and the River, which are well worth seeing.

Next morning, starting early, you will easil) or Wallingford on the first day ; on the seco' Sonning ; third, Marlow ; fourth, Windsor Moulsey ; sixth, Richmond or Wandsworth miles per day, and will give you time to pay most interesting spots on the river.

HENLEY,

HENLEY BRIDGE, from Oxford, 46 m. 7 fur. 53 yds. ; to Putney Bridge, 57 m. 4 fur. 13 yds.

HENLEY STATION (G.W.R., Henley Branch), about 2 fur. from the Bridge.

Henley is, according to Dr. Plot, the oldest town in Oxfordshire. Its scenery on all sides is very beautiful. The fine range of wooded hills that close the distance, mirrored in the clear and ample river, give it an indescribable charm. There is not much of note in the town of Henley besides the Bridge and Church. The Bridge is a fine stone structure of five arches, the keystone of the centre arch being ornamented by sculptured allegorical heads of Thames and Isis. The Church is a noble building in the Decorated style of architecture ; it has a lofty square turreted tower, said to have been designed or erected by Cardinal Wolsey. The entrance to Henley by the Oxford Road (called the " Fair Mile") is also very pleasing. Henley is well known to oarsmen, on account of the annual Regatta held here, established in 1839, which may be considered one of the most successful meetings of the kind held in England ; it is visited by the *élite* of the aquatic world, and during its continuance, the town is the centre of a very fashionable gathering.

The Course is from the Island below Fawley Court to near the Bridge, a distance of nearly a mile and three furlongs : one of the finest reaches on the river. Just above the bridge on the Berkshire side is a large boat-house, for housing the boats of competitors at the Regatta.

Boats housed or to be let.

Mrs. LAMBOURNE ; F. JOHNSON ; R. BEDWELL ; Mrs. HOOPER.

HOTELS.

The " Red Lion," (see p. 63), the " Angel (see p. 64.)
The " Catherine Wheel," the " White Ha

INNS.

The " Little White Hart," just below the the " Carpenters' Arms ;" the " Two Brewe others.

WATERMEN.

H. LAMBOURNE ; H. JONES ; E. VAUGI T. NEAL, jun. ; J. IVES.

Fishing.—The river about Henley is well spot for anglers of every class, who are allu beauties of the landscape. The water is fish, so, if the weather be favourable, a Henley is not to be despised.

FISHERMEN.

WILLIAM PARROTT ; EDWARD VAUGHAN EDWARD WOODLEY ; HENRY ALLUM ; GEO.

Bathing at the Henley Bathing Com[Solomon's Hatch ; also at Marsh Lock-poo

HAMBLEDON LOCK, from Henley Bridge to Medmenham Ferry, 2 m. o fur. 66 yds. ; to 4 ft. 8 in. in low water ; average in sumr

Inn at Aston, The " Flower-pot," (see p.

Fishing.—Above Hambledon Lock the r its Pike, and below, in the race, is a favour which are stated to reach a quarter of a por

H. W. TAUNT'S Agent at Henley : Mr. KIN
Market-place,

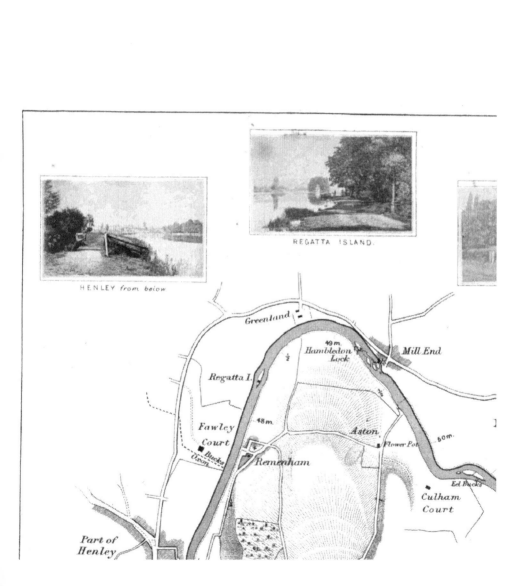

HENLEY *from below*

REGATTA ISLAND.

Greenland

49 m.
Hambledon
Lock

Mill End

½

Regatta I.

¾

48 m.

Fawley
Court

Aston.

Flower Pot

50 m.

Bucks
Oxon

Remenham

Ed Bucks

Culham
Court

Part of
Henley

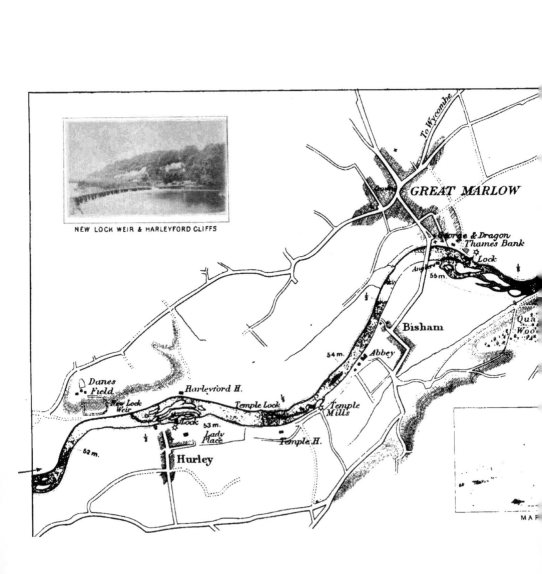

NEW LOCK WEIR & HARLEYFORD CLIFFS

To Wycombe

GREAT MARLOW

George & Dragon
Thames Bank

Lock

55 m.

Bisham

54 m.

Abbey

Danes
Field

Harleyford H.

New Lock
Weir

Temple Lock

Temple
Mills

Lock

53 m.

Lady
Place

Temple H.

Hurley

52 m.

Qua
Woo

MAP

MEDMENHAM.

MEDMENHAM FERRY, from Henley, 4 m. 2 fur. 101 yds. ; to Hurley Lock, 1 m. 4 fur. 168 yds.

Medmenham Abbey, close by, is well known by pleasure parties, being chosen as the favourite spot for picnicing by persons from Marlow and Maidenhead, as well as Henley. Medmenham was first built as an offshoot to the monastery of Woburn in Bedfordshire, and as such existed for about 200 years. It was afterwards annexed to Bisham Abbey. During the last century it acquired great notoriety as the meeting-place of a club of *débauchés* of rank and fashion : of their doings it would be unwise to speak, but the motto over the doorway sufficiently shews the class of men, "*Fay ceque Voudras*" ("Each as he likes.") The Abbey, with its ivy-mantled walls, is an interesting object; and its effect is heightened by the addition of a modern antique tower, &c., corresponding with the style of the other building.

Hotel.—The "Ferry," close to the Abbey. (See p. 64.)

In the village of Medmenham, the top of the hill is crowned by an old farmhouse, said to be mentioned in Domesday Book; whilst the Church nestles itself in the valley below ; a few fine old English cottages stand near the foreground, completing the picture. Not far below Medmenham we come to a bold bluff on the left bank ; and just below (in high water), a dangerous weir, or overfall, *which directly faces the centre of the stream;* the proper course is near the right bank. At Danesfield, near here, are the remains of an encampment attributed to the Danes.

HURLEY.

HURLEY LOCK, from Medmenham Ferry, to Temple Lock, 5 fur. 23 yds. : average f does not vary much.

HURLEY, on the right bank just above the passed by without a visit. There are the · a Monastery (Lady Place) founded in the Çonqueror ; the Church being entire, and t preservation ; the ancient refectory is convert by are the remains of the vaults of the man by Lord Lovelace in 1600 ; they are intere place where measures were entered into for in of Orange, which led to the Revolution of were held under cover of a round of splen it is stated that the most important pape recess at one end of the vault. On the o ford House, the residence of Sir Wm. Clayto at the foot of its hanging woods.

Fishing.—The' reaches here, both up an Chub and Pike, and at the Weir are fine P below Medmenham are fine swims, and fr Culham Court the water is deep and teemin

TEMPLE LOCK, from Hurley, 5 fur. 23 yds 1 m. 3 fur. 201 yds. : falls from 2 ft. 3 in. in low water ; average in summer, about 4 ft

Passing Temple we soon come to BISHAM and old Norman Church peeping out betw Abbey, the seat of G. H. Vansittart, Esq., k of Stephen to the Knights Templars; but of that order, a priory was founded for Augus wards passed into the hands of the Bened

pressed with the rest of the monasteries. The present house was partly built by Sir Edward Hoby, about 1592. It is a fine building with centre tower, also cloisters on one side, and contains a fine Hall. The Church is crowded with monuments to personages of high· rank in times long gone by, including among others one to the memory of Richard Neville, the celebrated "King Maker."

MARLOW.

MARLOW BRIDGE, from Temple Lock, 1. m. 3 fur. 201 yds.; to Cookham Bridge, 3 m. 7 fur. 158 yds.

MARLOW LOCK, 1 fur. 107 yds. beyond the bridge: falls from 1 ft. 6 in. in high to 6 ft. in low water; average in summer, about 5 ft. 6 in.

RAILWAY STATION, Marlow-road (G. W. R., Wycombe Branch), distance about 3½ miles. A line to Marlow is in progress.

MARLOW is very prettily situated, but has nothing in itself calling for notice excepting the graceful Suspension-bridge and Weir. The Church, which is built on the site of a far prettier one, forms a conspicuous object with every view of the bridge. The river, soon after passing here, reaches the Bisham Woods, which stretch along the hills, and form a pleasing feature in the landscape. Pretty shaded walks stretch through them; and one bold bluff, from which a splendid view of Marlow and the neighbouring country is obtained, has a tragical legend attached to it. The river follows the hills nearly to Cookham, and then leaves them to join the glorious Cleveden Woods.

Boats housed and to be let.

JAS. HAINES,
ROBERT SHAW, } above the bridge.
MISS COMPIERE, at the "Anglers."
Houseboat to let, R. HARDING.

HOTELS.

The "Anglers," close to the bridge.
The "Crown."

INNS.

The "George and Dragon."
The "Barge Pole."
The "Two Brewers."

Fishing.—The fishing all round Marlo
I had the pleasure myself, this year, of se
8 lbs., that had been caught just this side o
A stuffed one, said to have been the h
Thames, hangs in one of the rooms of tl
taken by Robert Shaw. The waters are pr
and Cookham Angling Protection Socie
Robert, or Bob Shaw (as he is called) will
give any information. He lives in a new-
the bridge.

FISHERMEN.

ROBERT SHAW.
WM. SHAW.
GEO. WHITE.
T. WHITE.
JEM WHITE.
WM. ROCKWELL.
H. ROCKWELL.

Fish.—Trout, Pike, Perch, Gudgeon, Ro

Bathing at the Weir, from the "Anglers;"

Henry W. TAUNT'S Agent for Marlow : Mr. SMIT!

THAMES CONSERVANCY BYE-LAWS.

THE following are the principal of the new bye-laws of the Conservancy relating to the pleasure-traffic on the river Thames :—

No steam-vessel shall be worked or navigated upon the river Thames between Teddington Lock, in the parish of Ham, in the County of Surrey, and Cricklade, in the county of Wilts, at such speed as shall endanger or cause any injury to the banks of the river.

Tolls for ferries each time of crossing, are—

For a horse not engaged in towing, taken across by ferry-boat, 3d.

For a horse and carriage, 6d.

For two horses and a carriage, 1s.

For foot-passengers, each 1d.

The following are the pleasure-boat tolls for locks :—

For every steam pleasure-boat, not exceeding 35ft. in length, 9d. ; for every steam pleasure-boat exceeding 35ft. in length, for every additional 5 ft. of length, 3d.

Class 1.—For every pair-oared row-boat, skiff, out-rigger, randan, dinghy, punt, canoe, or company boat, 3d.

Class 2.—For every four-oared row-boat, (other than the boats enumerated in Class 1,) 6d.

Class 3.—For every row-boat, shallop, and company boat, over four oars, 9d.

For every house-boat, 2s. 6d.

The above charges to be for passing once through the lock, and returning the same day.

The following are the annual tolls. In lieu of the above tolls, pleasure steamboats or row-boats may be registered on the annual payment to the Conservators of the undermentioned sums, and shall, in consideration of such payment, pass the several locks free of any other charge :—

For every steam pleasure-boat not exceeding 35 ft. in length, 40s. per annum, with 5s. extra for every additional 5 ft.

For every row-boat of Class 1, 20s. per annum.

For every row-boat of Class 2, 30s. per annum.

For every row-boat of Class 3, 40s. per annum.

For every house-boat, 100s. per annum.

CONVEYANCE OF BOATS BY

LONDON AND SOUTH-WESTER

THIS Company's rates for BOATS conveyed l as follows :—If requiring one carriage-truck, th a four-wheeled carriage ; if two trucks are req for two four-wheeled carriages. The crew, if tr 1d. per mile, provided that not less than four pa CANOES will be charged the same rate, as a ge veyed between two terminal stations, and the top of a carriage with convenience and safety prepared to charge a reduced rate ; but all sucl of special arrangement, and be dealt with as th

GREAT WESTERN RAIL

Boats and Canoes conveyed in the guard's va ordinary passenger-carriage are charged 2d. per with a minimum charge of 5s., at owner's risk canoes are so large as to require a special truc is as follows :—When one truck or carriage is : as for one private carriage ; when two trucks a and-a-half private carriages ; when three trucl two private carriages ; when four trucks are re a-half private carriages. In cases where the c in number) travel with the boat, the charge latter will be reduced one-half, in all cases by owner's risk.

BONE END AND MARLOW-ROAD.

RAILWAY STATION, Marlow-road (G. W. R.), 3 fur. from landing-place.

Inn, "Railway Tavern," close to the Station.

Boats to let, A. P. SPEECHLEY.

Fisherman, GEO. HOLLAND.

COOKHAM AND CLEVEDEN.

COOKHAM BRIDGE, from Marlow Lock, 3 m. 6 fur. 51 yds.; to Cleveden Ferry, 7 fur. 154 yds.

STATION, COOKHAM (G. W. R., Wycombe Branch), 5 fur. from the bridge.

A short distance above Cookham the Thames is joined by the Wyke. Cookham Church stands near the river, and forms a picturesque object from it. The river is crossed here by a slim iron bridge, and just below is divided into a number of streams, Hedsor is in sight, and the old Folly on the hill attracts attention; but just below is Cleveden, the finest reach on the Thames. Passing down the Cut and through the Lock, we reach the overhanging woods, and turning short round, glide tranquilly along the river at their base. The scenery here is the grandest on the river, but it is impossible to give any adequate description of it : it must be seen. The mind of every one is so entranced with its loveliness that details cannot be entered into, but all is summed up in the one expression, "How beautiful!" Cleveden House is built on the summit of the hill, and the view from its terrace is unequalled. The mansion was first erected by Geo. Villiers, Duke of Buckingham. Frederick, Prince of Wales, the father of George III., had it for some time as his summer residence; and it was whilst here that the masque of "Alfred" was performed. It was composed by Thomson, but is nearly forgotten except

one song which is immortal,—"Rule Brita be lost. Villiers' house was destroyed by mansion—designed by Barry—erected in in the possession of the Marquis of Westmi

The scenery the whole of the distance to not equally grand, still retains enough of it a longing for a nearer view.

The island of Formosa lies on the oppos Woods, just above the Ferry.

HOTELS, (at Cookha
The "Ferry Hotel," close to the bridge.
The "King's Arms," in the village. (Se
Inn, The "Bel and Dragon."

Boats to be let and hou
W. LACEY; R. POULTON.

Fishing.—Cookham Reach is a splendid w and Jack; and it is very seldom that, in see a number of anglers in their punts, n teristic way of the Thames. Below, under the water is still good; and pitches may be then the whole distance to Boulter's Weir.

FISHERMEN.

EDWARD GODDING; JEM DREWETT; HAR enhead, generally here in the season).

Splendid bathing at Odney Weir.

COOKHAM LOCK, to Boulter's Lock, 1 falls from 1 ft. 6 in. in high to 5 ft. in lo summer, about 4 ft.

BOULTER'S LOCK, from Cleveden Ferry, to Maidenhead Bridge, 5 fur. 70 yds. : fall: 7 ft. in low water; average in summer, abou

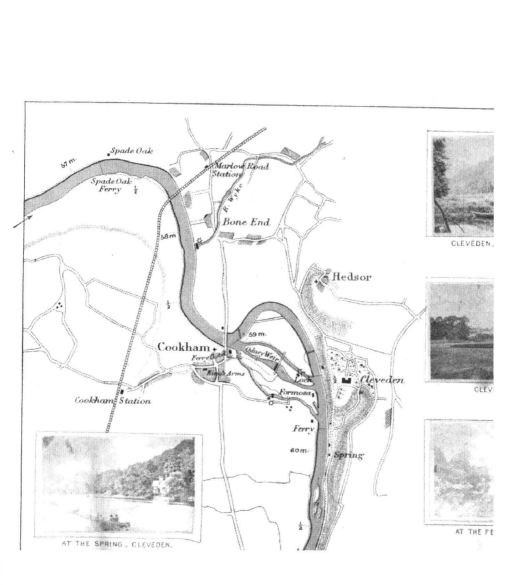

Spade Oak

57 m.

Spade Oak
Ferry ½

Marlow Road
Station

R. Wye

Bone End

58 m.

Hedsor

Cookham

½

59 m.

Olney Weir

Ferry
Kings Arms

Lock

Formosa

Cleveden

Cookham Station

Ferry

60 m.

Spring

½

CLEVEDEN.

CLEV

AT THE FE

AT THE SPRING . CLEVEDEN.

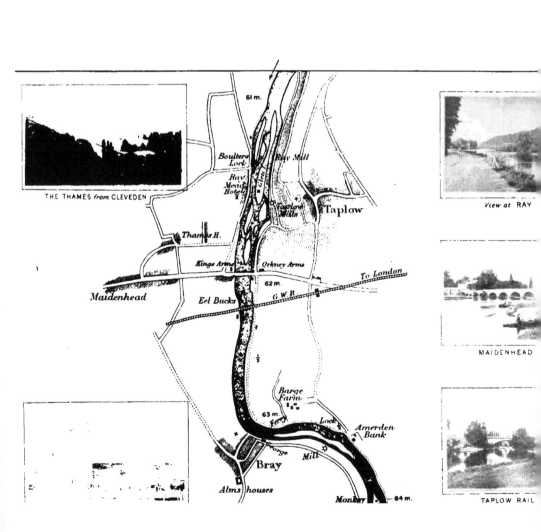

THE THAMES *from* CLEVEDEN

61 m.

Boulters
Lock

Ray Mill

Ray
Mead
Hotel

Glen

Taplow
Mills

Taplow

Thames H.

Kings Arms

Orkney Arms

Maidenhead

Eel Bucks

62 m.

To London

G.W.R.

½

Barge
Farm

63 m.

Lock

Amerden
Bank

Gorge

Mill

Bray

Alms houses

Monkey

64 m.

View at RAY

MAIDENHEAD

TAPLOW RAIL

MAIDENHEAD.

MAIDENHEAD BRIDGE, from Boulter's Lock, 5 fur. 70 yds. ; to Bray Lock, 1 m. 3 fur. 152 yds.

The London road, from the West of England, passes over this bridge. Maidenhead stands some distance from the river, and consists mostly of one long street, but there is nothing of any consequence to attract the visitor: Maidenhead depends upon Cleveden for its interest. Taplow Bridge, just below Maidenhead, is celebrated for the enormous span of its arches, being the largest in the world composed of brick only ; one of Brunel's grand designs. About four miles from Maidenhead is a celebrated resort of pic-nic parties, called Burnham Beeches, where, under magnificent old trees, gnarled and rugged, many a pleasant holiday is spent. For the artist there are days of intense enjoyment amongst their weird groupings,

Stations near Maidenhead Bridge.

MAIDENHEAD STATION (G. W. R.), about a mile from the river.

HOTELS.

"Ray Mead," close to Boulter's Lock, (see p. 61).
"Thames Hotel."
Skindle's "Orkney Arms" Hotel. (See p. 67).
"King's Arms," all near the river. (See p. 64.)
"Red Lion."
"White Hart," and others, in Maidenhead.

INNS, (in Maidenhead).

"Saracen's Head ;" "White Horse ;" "Swan," &c.

H. W. TAUNT'S Agent at Maidenhead: Mr. HODGES, Stationer.

W. DEACON.
*H. WOODHOUSE, "Ray Mead" Hotel.
*J. BOND, close to the bridge.
S. ROSE.

Boats housed and to b

Ponies for towing, at W. Deacon's, "Ra

Fishing.—The fishing to Boulter's Lock there are also several good swims for Gu bridge Jack and Perch abound ; whilst al of the osier-beds are Chub in great force be met with.

FISHERMEN.

HY. WILDER.
ED. ANDREWS.
RD. ANDREWS.
GEO. SAUNDERS.
J. SIMMONS.
MARK ANDREWS.

Fish.—Trout, Jack, Perch, Chub, 1 Gudgeon, &c.

Bathing at Boulter's Weir.

BRAY.

BRAY LOCK, from Maidenhead Bridge to Monkey Island, 4 fur. 128 yds. : open fall in summer, about 1 ft. 9 in.

BRAY has no scenery to boast of; but it from the memory of its "vivacious Vic king did reign, would still be Vicar of will repay a visit : the old houses round also are worth notice. The Alms-house Bray, ought not to be missed.

CAMPING OUT, No. 2.—(IN A BOAT.)

BY THE EDITOR.

"THAT'S just what I should like!"—"How jolly it must be!"—"Well, you must enjoy yourself!"—"I don't wonder at your looking so well!"—"Ain't you afraid to go to sleep?" These remarks, and fifty others, were passed one evening amongst a circle of friends to whom I had been relating my experiences in camping out. I had just returned from a tour on the Thames, extending over a little more than three months; and I could echo one of the exclamations above by answering, "It *is* jolly." I think, too, it will be re-echoed by numbers of persons who have tried it, and thoroughly enjoyed themselves. There are, perhaps, a number of reasons why camping out should be enjoyable. First, we live in an age so fast and energetic, that the mind and body get thoroughly used up, demanding in the same interval rest and renewal of vigour, that may fit for after periods of toil; and what greater pleasure can there be to a man tired out in body and mind, than to throw himself on his back under some wide-spreading tree, and listen to the gentle stream that murmurs by? or, with rod in hand, to watch the nodding float which, in disappearing, rouses him from a pleasant reverie? And again, the custom of our age is so polite and graceful as to be at times a positive tax upon a man's time and person, making, by contrast, a wild life enjoyable; in fact, the ennui that often takes possession of us would entirely disappear if we were not so highly civilized.

Not that civilization, in its present state, is a failure—far from it; still it is at times a boon to be able to lay aside the conventionalities of society, and our glimpse of nomadic life forms one of those complementary tones which, in a picture, harmonize and give vigour to the whole composition.

It is just the opposite to our usual life; and this is just the reason why camping out is so much liked b[y]
They leave behind them those cares of [t]
accounts, those toils of pleasure that tur[n]
in a more simple manner and style, they [...]
food and their rest.

Secondly, camping out is enjoyed be[...]
more robust health. Excesses of every kind
and this also is one of the causes of lassitu[de]
I speak of excesses, I do not mean altoget[her]
and drinking, or worse, I mean the ordinar[y]
a business man meets.

To labour for hours in a foul atmospher[e]
men in London do, is an excess that da[...]
and would more, perhaps, were it not the [...]
from town to spend the night in a purer a[ir]
every nerve of the brain in getting off orde[rs]
the shortest space of time possible, and wi[th]
the slightest detail; or to be perched at a [...]
accounts day after day, with scarcely th[e]
posture; all these are excesses that every [...]
meets with, and which make the health o[f]
cate. I might go on and complete the ca[...]
working merchants of our capital will we[...]
my going further.

Gentlemen, too, who have no busine[ss]
growing on their time and selves; what [...]
the midnight party or dance? and how oft[en]
or some other such tonic is required. Cam[...]
for these, more robust health, sounder sle[ep]
ment, than anything I know at the same co[st]

Ah, there's the *third* reason—cost! There are pleasures that force their memory on some of us in consequence of the deprivation they entail. Camping out does not do this. If properly managed, the cost of the requisite kit is more than saved by the comparatively small expense with which the journey is attended. Perhaps some of the hotel-keepers will not thank me for pursuing this subject; but I am trying to open the river for all, and must tell what I know. I have nothing to say against a single landlord; I know a great many of them, and number some amongst my friends: I am also of opinion that, instead of injuring them, I shall help to do them good; such is, at least, my wish. Hotels cannot be otherwise than expensive, to a certain extent; they usually have an enormous quantity of out-goings, and in consequence are obliged to recoup themselves; but at the same time I know a great many on the Thames that are thoroughly moderate, and keep down their charges as far as they can. I might go still further, and speak of kindnesses that I know of that have been done, things that would redound to their honour; but it would be unfair to the rest to single out one or two, so I must refrain. However, to our subject. The cost of camping is much less than hotels, as there need be no expenses beyond the necessaries of life, and these are bought first hand. Of course it is an easy thing to make camping out as expensive, or even more so, than living at the hotels. Just go to Fortnum and Mason, or some other purveyors, and order them to send you down a hamper of the greatest delicacies every day, and you will find camping out anything but cheap: you had better go to an Hotel. Of course pastry and so on are very nice, they relish now and then first class after the well-cooked fish and steak; but—as a rule—if you camp out much, you will rather depend upon what you can do yourself.

There are in the market, at the present time, so many delicacies in a portable form, that one scarcely needs the help of the confectioner otherwise in the camp; and in case such a change

is wished for, one can always go to an hotel
time further in proving what I think is pat
why do we have so many pic-nic parties?)
thoroughly enjoyable; nay, more, that it is
cheapest pleasures a man can have; but will
tion to another side of the question, the diffi
There are two principal modes of camping at
the river Thames, and they differ mostly in t
ments. The one is to sleep on the shore t
other to sleep in the boat, arranged at night fc
prefer the latter; but that ideas on both s
should be given, I have induced a gentleman
deal of his time in tent life on the river, to
on the subject. The only one advantage th
has over the boat is, that a narrower, smalle
but there are a number of things to be stated
way. I must confess I have never tried a t
have seen my arrangement have left their
boats arranged for sleeping on my plan, w
and does not involve any very great expense
is termed in Oxford phrase, a Company bo
gig with side-seats from the back rail, and a
up and down); a locker for food was fitted l
The boat is about 18 ft. long and 4 ft. 6 in.
part, and is fitted with the usual mast at the
close to the rudder-post, another short mast i
for a flag-staff during the day. When arrangi
ing is raised and fastened, then a side coverin
secured with strings all round to the iron whi
and fixed below the seats of the boat with lo
completely enclosing the middle part of the
side seats we place boards fitted on purpo
side seats, under the cushions, in the day-tim

BRAY (continued).

INNS.

The "George," close to the river. (See p. 67.)
The "Hind's Head," in the village.

Boats housed and to be let.

*W. WOODHOUSE, at the "George" Inn.

Fishing.—The fishing round Bray is good for Jack, Perch, and Gudgeon ; Barbel are found at the Weir and in the stream near Monkey Island ; and Chub exist nearly everywhere, under the shelving banks on the one side of the river, and the ozier beds on the other.

FISHERMEN.

W. WOODHOUSE.
J. CHAPMAN.
J. CHAPMAN, jun.

Bathing at the Weir.

Inn at Amerden Bank (just below Bray Lock), and punts to let.

MONKEY ISLAND AND HOTEL.

From MAIDENHEAD BRIDGE, 2 m. 0 fur. 60 yds. ; to Windsor Bridge, 4 m. 4 fur. 90 yds.

MONKEY ISLAND received its name from a pleasure-house built on it by the third Duke of Marlborough, the ceiling of which is adorned with paintings of monkeys e1 sports. The house is now formed into an i by pleasure parties and anglers, the "mon in good preservation, and the fishing all r(The stream from Bray Lock past here to t on the Thames.

Fishing punts to let.

Fisherman, R. PLUMMER, jun.

Bathing from the island.

SURLEY HALL. Inn, (no beds). This fishing resort by parties from Windsor ; for the Eton boys, and where, in a mead(their annual College festival on the fourth above is Water Oakley Court, a fine man: style. The fishing all round here for Pik Gudgeon, is thoroughly good, particularly i as Eykyn's Pool, near the Willows.

BOVENEY LOCK, from Monkey Island, 2 Bridge, 1 m. 7 fur. 90 yds. : falls from 2 f\ in low water ; average in summer, 3 ft. 9 ir

Bathing at the Weir ; also at Athens, Eton boys are away for the vacation, in Au

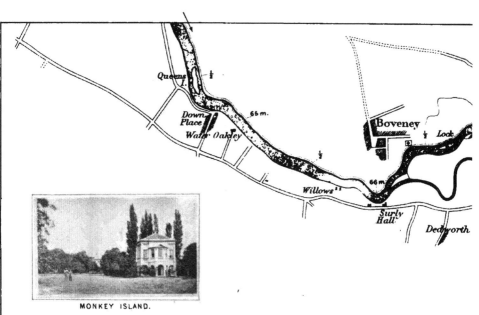

Queens

Down Place

Water Oakley

66 m.

Boveney

Lock

Willows

66 m.

Surly Hall

Dedworth

MONKEY ISLAND.

WINDSOR *from the* BROCAS

CLEWER CHURCH.

ETON
College
Lock
69m.
Black Potts
Victoria B.
Christopher
Crown
Brocas
S.W.R.
Station
Datchet
Little
70m.
Royal
Station
G.W.R.
Castle
Park
Barracks
WINDSOR
S.W.R.
Frogmore
Southley
71m.
Albert B.
Weir
Cut
Long Walk
Farm
Old
Windsor
Lock

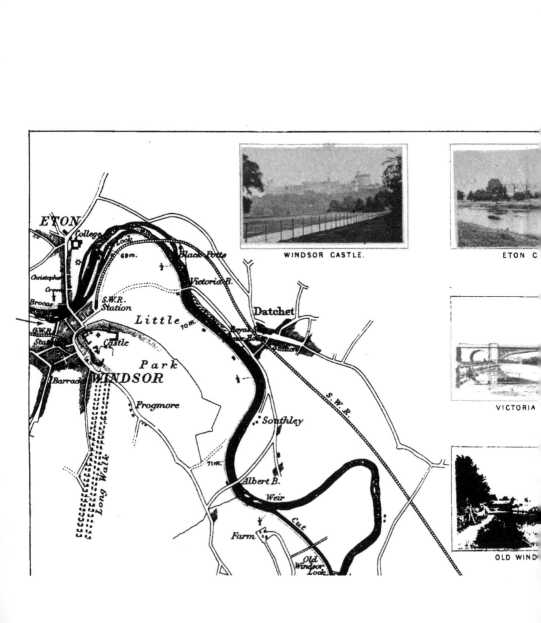

WINDSOR CASTLE.

ETON C

VICTORIA

OLD WIND

WINDSOR AND ETON.

WINDSOR BRIDGE, from Boveney Lock, 1 m. 7 fur. 90 yds.; to Romney Lock, 3 fur. 96 yds.

At Boveney Lock we catch the first good peep of the Royal Castle of Windsor; and all the way on we get pleasant views every now and then; till, passing under the Great Western Railway Bridge, it bursts upon us in all its splendour. The view of Windsor from the Brocas is the grandest on the River Thames. It should be seen with the red light of sunset glinting upon it; then the warm lights, contrasting so finely with the cold grey shadows, make every part stand out with boldness and reality; and the noble round tower, raising its head far above the surrounding buildings, gives a breadth and airiness to the whole. The Curfew, or Julius Cæsar's Tower, a building of huge proportions, was altered under the direction of His late Royal Highness the Prince Consort; but from whatever point we view the western façade, its exceeding beauty and exquisite harmony of proportion are marred by this vast Belfry Tower. Windsor Castle was commenced by William the Conqueror, who turned the neighbouring country into a royal forest, and used the house as a hunting-lodge. By Henry I. it was rebuilt, and here it was he celebrated his second marriage. In the time of Stephen, the age of castles, it was reckoned second in the kingdom. Edward III. was born here, and we owe the greater part of this splendid palace to him. He appointed William of Wykeham surveyor of the works, and had the workmen impressed from the surrounding counties. After Edward III., Windsor, for near a century, received no addition, until Edward IV. erected St. George's Chapel, perhaps the most exquisite specimen of the architecture of that period which exists. Elizabeth caused the north terrace to be constructed, from which is seen one of the finest views on the whole of the river. Shakespeare wrote his comedy of the "Merrie Wives of Windsor" at her command, and it was performed b
The Castle has undergone immense restoı
since 1824, particularly by King George
of Sir Jeffery Wyattville, the architect.

It is thrown open to visitors when
Guides, with every information requir
mittance can be obtained of Mr. Colli
my agent at Windsor. The views of the
park, and also from Eton, are very fine; l
to that from the Brocas.

RAILWAY STATI

The G. W. R. (Branch), High-street; tl
line), 1¾ mile distant; the S.W.R., Datch

Boats housed and to l

* J. and S. SALTER, * H. GOODMAN, Et

HOTELS.

The "White Hart" (see p. 68); the "C
and the "Star and Garter," (the site of t
"Merrie Wives of Windsor,") at Windso
at Eton.

INNS.

The "Crown and Cushion," Eton, (see
The "New Inn," Eton-square; the "
"Royal Oak," at Windsor.

H. W. TAUNT'S Agent at Windsor: Mr. COLL
DRAKE, High-street.

Fishing.—Just below Boveney Weir, wh
streams meet, there is capital bank-fish
Bucks side of the river; and at lower H
many Barbel are found. In Clewer Mil

taken, there is also excellent Chub-fishing at the exit of the water at Dead Water Eyot; and from thence under the boughs down stream for a quarter of a mile quantities are caught, whipping with large artificial flies, either Bees, or Palmers. A little above the G.W.R. Bridge on the Windsor side is a capital Gudgeon pitch. Good bank-fishing for Roach is had from the Brocas shore, about fifty yards from the magnificent clump of elms; quantities are also captured at the back of the "Fireworks Eyot," on which is the grand pyrotechnic display at the Eton Festival on the fourth of June.

Below Windsor Bridge some fine Trout are always taken each season, and from Eton Weir to the Playing-fields, for about half-a-mile, is a famous Trout stream, in which some spotted beauties sport, and are often captured from the island. ."New Works Hole," opposite "Sixth Form Bench," where the best cricketers of the school have tea on summer evenings, is a famous deep for Barbel; while at "the Needles," that "meeting of the waters" where the different streams divided by Romney Island unite and mingle in exceeding loveliness, is one of the choicest spots for punt-fishing on the entire Thames; it is much frequented by London anglers. The only other noticeable spots in the Windsor and Eton district is "Hog Hole," about 300 yards above Victoria Bridge, in mid-stream; it is of great depth, and full of Dace, Chub, and Barbel, with an occasional Trout.

Fishing-tackle Manufacturer, ROBERT SMITH, Eton, close to Windsor Bridge.

FISHERMEN.

GEO. HOLLAND ("Nottingham George"), assistant river-keeper; CHAS. BREACH; J. MAYSEY; JEM BRYAN;. G. PLUMRIDGE; GEORGE LAMB; GEORGE HILL.

Fish.—Barbel, Chub, Roach, Pike, Trout, Gudgeon, Perch, Dace, &c.

Bathing. At Athens, on the main stream.

Windsor Bathing-place (by subscription) Windsor side.

Cuckoo Weir, a branch of the Thames of

Also at Eton Weir.

ROMNEY LOCK, from Windsor Bridge, 3 toria Bridge, 6 fur. 34 yds.

ETON COLLEGE stands near the river, near Lock: the view from this point is one of the from the north terrace of the Castle. Eton by King Henry VI., in 1440. It still contin of the scholarships at King's College, Camb 70 students annually to the two Universiti a graceful exterior in the Perpendicular s being equally chaste; it contains severa windows, two of which are in memory of t in the Crimean war. The other buildings and not fine as specimens of architectu number of our most celebrated men have among others, Wellington, Canning, Gray, and Gladstone.

Below Eton we pass, for the first time, South-Western Railway, by an elegant gi after reach Victoria, the first of the twin via the Home-park. They are said to have bee Albert, and the land between them being property, none but persons towing a boat or horse are allowed to be on shore. Herne Shakespeare, which stood hard by, and form attraction, was blown down during a sumr day of August, 1863. On the other bank "mead" will be remembered as the scene ducking in the Thames; and of which su so feelingly--"that drowning swells a man.'

DATCHET.

FROM this spot a pontoon bridge has been twice erected for the passage of troops by thousands, when there have been royal reviews in Windsor Great-park. There are, on the green, a few old English houses, but nothing else worthy of note, the Church having been newly restored in a style too modern to suit an English village landscape.

Boats to let.

JAS. COX.
JAS. HOARE.

HOTELS.

"Manor Hotel," (see p. 67.)
"Royal Stag."
Inn, "Morning Star."

RAILWAY STATION (S. E. R.), about 2 fur. from river.

Fishing.—At "Swan's Bridge," almost joining Albert Bridge, where the drain from Windsor Castle and the Barracks empties itself into the river, Roach and Dace, particularly the former, are caught literally by thousands : there is nothing in the whole course of the Thames equal to the immense number taken here by anglers ; and there are often a dozen punts engaged at a time in the successful, but not over-sweet, occupation. As the stream is bordered by the private part of the Home-park, angling is only permitted here from boats.

In our notice of the fishing spots in this portion of our river, it is only necessary further to mention the well-known "Coln-brook Churchyard," situated in the old river at Old Windsor, about a quarter of a mile below the Weir, where hundreds of large Barbel and Chub are taken. The place is so named from a popular legend that, in the beginning of the seventeenth cen-tury, when highwaymen infested the main London-road from Hounslow Heath to Colnbrook, and Claud great captain of the band, the bodies of all their lives in the frequent deadly encounter night to this place, heavily weighted in sacl the Thames. It is a fact that a short time ag that had been evidently long embedded in covered here by some ballast-heavers.

FISHERMEN.

GEO. KEEN ; —. PEARCE ; GEO. BAILEY ;

OLD WINDSOR LOCK, from Albert Bridge Magna Charta Island, 1 m. 3 fur. : falls from 6 in. in low water ; average in summer, abou

The river, after leaving the Albert Bridge, f the new Weir : the boat-track being the cut At Old Windsor Lock are some new Wate supplying the Castle, &c.

THE "Bells of Ouseley," a noted Inn on th seven furlongs below, in a very pleasant n there is fishing in abundance. The county o river just below here.

Boats to let, WILLIAM HAYNES.

Fisherman, WILLIAM HAYNES.

MAGNA CHARTA ISLAND, from Old Winds to Bell Weir Lock, 1 m. 3 fur. 157 yds.

MAGNA CHARTA ISLAND is well known to history as being the place where, on the 19t Barons forced King John to sign the docu Great Charter of England, and which has bor that forms the birthright of every Englishm said to have been signed upon a stone, whi a table in the cottage. On the other side of the river is Runnymede. Ankerwycke, just below, is also historical. Henry VIII. is said to have wooed Anne Boleyn under a yew-tree still in existence, and also to have waited there for the signal following her execution. Ankerwycke House stands near the ruins of a priory of Benedictine nuns, founded by Sir Gilbert Montfichet, the owner of the manor in the reign of Henry II.

Cooper's Hill, on the other side of the river, forms part of the elevated range which encloses the view. It is well known from Denham's poem, of which the following is a specimen :—

> "My eye, descending from this hill, surveys
> Where Thames among the wanton valley strays :—
> Thames, the most loved of all the ocean's sons
> By his old sire, to his embraces runs,—
> Hasting to pay his tribute to the sea ;
> Like mortal life to meet eternity.
>
> * * * * *
>
> . . . . Godlike his unwearied bounty flows ;
> First loves to do, then loves the good he does."

Fishing.—Close to the "Bells" is a good place for Gudgeon, where they are to be found in large quantities ; and from here right down below Ankerwycke, is first-class water for trolling and Roach-fishing. Barbel find a home close to Magna Charta Island, and also at the Bell Weir ; whilst under the boughs on the Buckinghamshire side, Perch and Chub are to be found.

BELL WEIR LOCK, Egham, from Magna Charta Island, 1 m. 3 fur. 157 yds. ; to Staines Bridge, 7 fur. 195 yds. : falls from 1 ft. in high to 6 ft. in low water ; average in summer, about 5 ft.

EGHAM stands on the south side of the river, not far from Bell Weir. Its Church, which is excessively plain, contains monuments to Sir John Denham and his two wives.

Inn at Bell Weir Lock, the "Angler's Rest." (See p. 68.)

Boats to let and housed, E. HAWKES, ("Angler's Rest.")

H. W. TAUNT'S Agent at EGHAM: Mr. LARKIN, Stationer.

RAILWAY STATION, Egham (S. W. R., R 5 fur. from the river.

HOTELS, (at Egha The "Catherine Wheel ;" the "King's H

FISHERMEN.

JAMES KEEN ; EDWARD WELLBELOVED.

Ferry to Wraysbury.

STAINES

JUST above Staines, the river Colne ent Close to one stands "London Stone," the bo of Middlesex and Buckinghamshire, and ancient jurisdiction of the city of London up the top of the original stone was inscribe City of London, A.D. 1280," some of wh legible. Staines Bridge is of white granite, the failure of several attempts to construct town, but has nothing to call for notice, e near the Church, called Duncroft, said to I King John's ; but the house scarcely dates the Elizabethan style. It has a large bre factories of Linoleum floor-cloth.

RAILWAY STATION (S. W. R.), some di through the town ; branches from here to V

Hotel, the "Angel and Crown," High-stre

INNS.

The "Swan ;" the "Pack-horse," (see Inn ;" the "White Lion ;" the "Ship."

Boats to be let and hou
*HENRY VEARS, (near the church, s CAMBERS ; H. LEACH, near the bridge.

H. W. TAUNT'S Agent at Staines: Mr. WA

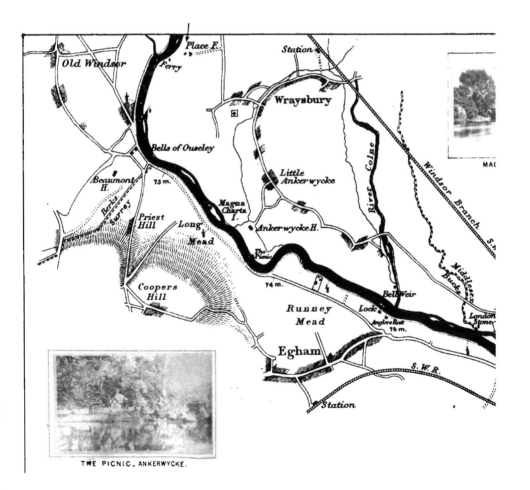

Place F.

Old Windsor

Ferry

Station

Wraysbury

Bells of Ouseley

Beaumont
H.

73 m.

Little
Ankerwycke

River Colne

Windsor Branch S...

MAG...

Priest
Hill

Long
Mead

Magna
Charta
I.

Ankerwycke H.

Coopers
Hill

The
Picnic

74 m.

Bell Weir

Lock

Middlesex
Bucks

Runney
Mead

Anglers Rest
75 m.

London
Stone

Egham

S.W.R.

Station

THE PICNIC. ANKERWYCKE.

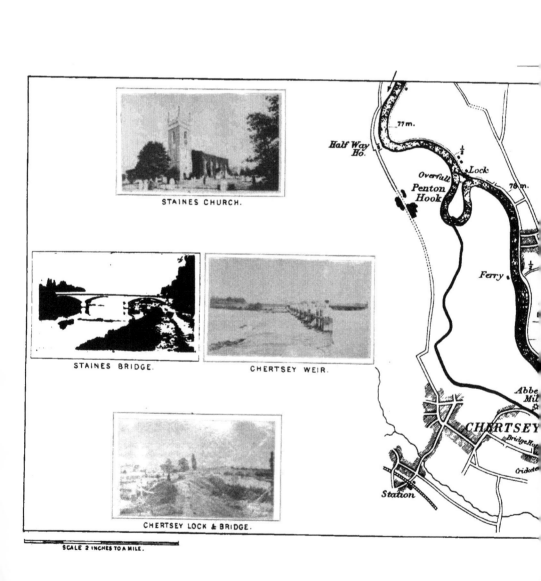

STAINES CHURCH.

STAINES BRIDGE.

CHERTSEY WEIR.

CHERTSEY LOCK & BRIDGE.

77 m.

Half Way Ho.

Overfall

Penton Hook

Lock

78 m.

Ferry

Abbey Mill

CHERTSEY

Bridge Ho

Oridote

Station

SCALE 2 INCHES TO A MILE.

Fishing.—At Staines Bridge there is excellent Barbel-fishing, and from the bank close by, just below where the drain from the brewery enters, is Roach and Gudgeon-fishing. In the back-water Perch are to be found, and above London Stone a fly will generally secure fine Chub. At Bell Weir Lock are some excellent swims. Below Staines bridge is a good Roach swim, and a little further down, close where the old bridge used to stand, is a noted swim for Barbel. Along the towing-path, still further on, is very respectable bank-fishing, whilst at Truss's Island are Perch and Roach.

FISHERMEN.

HENRY VEARS; THOS. FLETCHER; WM. CAMBERS; HY. AMOR; GEO. NIXON.

Bathing at Vears's Bathing-house, near the Church.

PENTON HOOK LOCK, from Staines Bridge, 1 m. 6 fur. 168 yds.; to Laleham Ferry, 6 fur. 140 yds.: falls, 2 ft. 6 in.; does not vary much.

Good bathing on the Hook.

LALEHAM.

LALEHAM FERRY, from Penton Hook Lock, 6 fur. 140 yds.; to Chertsey Lock, 1 m. 1 fur. 4 yds.

Laleham and Penton Hook are well known as splendid fishing localities, and are much frequented by anglers from London. It is, without exception, the best neighbourhood for fly-fishing on the Thames, and the takes are generally heavy.

To an angler camping out, this place offers unusual facilities; for, whilst he is in the midst of pleasant scenery and good fishing, he is close to a town where he can procure everything he may need, and the distance by the rail from London is less than an hour.

INNS.

The "Horse Shoes."
The "Feathers."

Boats to be let or housed, F. TROTTER, at Fe

FISHERMEN.

SAML. HARRIS; JOHN HARRIS; WM. HAR RIS; FRANK HARRIS; SAML. SCOTT.

Gentlemen who stop here often go into where are inns. (See under Chertsey.)

CHERTSEY

CHERTSEY LOCK, from Laleham Ferry, 1 Shepperton Lock, 1 m. 7 fur. 183 yds.: falls to 3 ft. 9 in. in low water; average in summer

CHERTSEY LOCK-HOUSE stands in Surrey Middlesex side of the river. Traces are still curved channel in which the Thames here ra being built the course of the stream was al Chertsey Bridge stands just below.

At the top part of the Weir-pool, the Tl a stream running from Penton Hook throug Chertsey. Chertsey is an ancient town, b antiquity in its appearance. It contains a Ch for its beauty, though scarcely so ugly as that other side of the Thames. The ancient imp was mainly owing to the noble Abbey, origin for the Benedictines. In the ninth centu destroyed by the Danes, who murdered the monks, ninety in number. Edgar, in 964, re the monastery. In 1010, the Saxon Chron

year men began to work at the new monastery at Chertsey."
The monastery prospered after this. It is said to have " covered
4 acres of ground, and looked like a town." The abbot wore the
mitre, was a baron, owing military service to the king, and had
privileges as wide as was customary with lord abbots. The do-
mains of the Abbey extended all along the side of the river, a long
way being a very fine meadow. They made a cut at the upper
end of it, which, taking in the waters of the river when it ap-
proached the Abbey, gained sufficient fall for a water-mill. Of
all this a fragment of wall, a rude gateway, part of a farm-house,
and the cut which still works a mill, are the sole remains.

Chertsey is also known from its connection with Cowley, the
poet, whose house still stands in Guildford-street. St. Anne's
Hill, near Chertsey, was the residence of Charles James Fox, the
noted politician. It is still a pleasant walk on a summer's day.

HOTELS.

"Chertsey Bridge Hotel," landing-stage just above the bridge.
The " Cricketers," close below the bridge. (See p. 69.)
The " Swan," the " Crown," in Chertsey.

INNS.

"Prince Regent," " King's Head," in Chertsey.

CHERTSEY STATION (S. W. R., Branch), Guildford-street, about
1½ mile from the Bridge.

FISHERMEN.

WM. GALLOWAY, sen. ; THOS. GALLOWAY, jun. ; JOHN KEEN ;
JAS. HASLETT ; JOHN POULTER ; THOS. TAYLOR ; —. TAYLOR, jun.

Fishing.—Below Chertsey Bridge, Trout, Dace, and Roach
abound, and good sport may be reckoned on ; also, nearing Shepperton, Jack and Chub take up their quarters, and are generally
to be found at home.

H. W. TAUNT'S Agents at Chertsey : KEMPSON and SON, Market-place.

WEYBRID

SHEPPERTON LOCK, from Chertsey Loc
to Halliford Point, 1 m. 2 fur. 33 yds. : fal
4 feet ; (very slow in emptying).

SHEPPERTON LOCK is situated on a sl
making a detour through the Weir. Wey
from the river up the back-water leadir
a long straggling place, boasting a monu
a very elegant new Church. The Wey joi
the upper being the navigable one, by
proceed to Guildford or Basingstoke.
Wey and Arun Canal, is now impractica
the abandonment of the navigation on it.
rather picturesque, and a few miles do
Newark Abbey, with its legend of the mor
under the Wey." The Waverley stream,
water, also joins here. The average fall
(mouth of the Wey), is about 9 feet.

Hotel, Weybridge, "Lincoln Arms," close

INNS.

"Queen's Head," " Ship," " King's Arr
in the village.

WEYBRIDGE STATION (S. W. R., Main I
from the river.

Boats housed and to b
J. HARRIS, "Lincoln Arms ;" E. KEEN

H. W. TAUNT'S Agent at Weybridge : M:

Fishing.—John Harris, of the "Lincoln Arms," tells me that "the reach from Chertsey Bridge to Shepperton is a very fine one for all kinds of fish : Chertsey scour is good for Trout and Dace ; Dumsey swim being a fine place for Barbel and Dace, and Dachet Point for Pike. At the back of Shepperton Weir, down to the landing for Weybridge, (the whole of the back-water leading up to the Weir,) is one of the finest streams for Trout we have about here." I merely add, that John Harris will be only too pleased to give any further information.

FISHERMEN.

J. Harris, W. House, "Lincoln Arms ;" W. Keen ; E. Keen ; A. Keen.

SHEPPERTON AND HALLIFORD.

Shepperton, like Weybridge, is a good deal resorted to by anglers. Jack, Perch, Chub, and Bream are to be found ; Barbel and other fish are also plentiful. This part of the river, right down to Richmond, is eminently a fishing as well as a pleasure resort, and where, on the upper stream, one sees a few bank anglers or a single punt in miles of distance, here they are everywhere to be met with, and form a feature in the landscape.

Hotel, Shepperton, the "Anchor." (See p. 70.)

INNS.

"King's Head."
"Rose and Crown."

Boats to be let or housed by G. and F. Purdue. (See p. 69.)

FISHERMEN.

Wm. Rogerson ; F. Purdue ; S. Purdue ; G. Rosewell ; C. Broadhead ; H. Purdue, jun.

Shepperton Station (S. W. R.), about a ɪ
Halliford Point, from Shepperton Lock to Walton Bridge, 6 fur. 156 yds.

HOTELS (Halliford
The "Ship." (See p. 70.)
The "Red Lion."

Inn, The "Crown."

*Boats to let by Thos. Rosewell.

FISHERMEN.

E. Rosewell ; T. Rosewell ; T. Purdu

WALTON-ON-TH

Walton Bridge, from Halliford Point, Sunbury Lock, 1 m. 5 fur. 130 yds.

A short distance before reaching here, ju stream, is a place known as Cowey Stakes, ford by which Cæsar crossed the Thames found here not many years back. Walton ł two sets of arches—is two bridges, in fact. some years ago, and is replaced by an ugl other *old* bridge, as it is called, is carried ove of ground, which, according to an old record of the Thames. Walton Church is an old str twelfth century. It contains, amongst others Shannon, by Roubilliac, and to William L Charles I. There is also a curious brass, the figure of a man riding on a stag, int plunging a sword. This person, (Selwyn,) on the back of a stag in the heat of the ch with his sword towards Queen Elizabeth, and when he came near her, plunged it into the animal's throat, so that he fell dead at her feet.

In the vestry is preserved one of those curious instruments, a scold's bit, the use of which was to make the offender hold her tongue.

Near Walton is Oatlands Park, once the favourite residence of Queen Elizabeth ; it is now turned into a magnificent hotel, and, still standing in its beautiful grounds, affords a residence surpassed by few of its competitors in England.

HOTELS.

"Oatlands' Park," (see p. 76); "Duke's Head," in Walton.

INNS.

The "Anglers," close to the river, (see p. 70); the "Old Manor House;" the "Crown," (see p. 71).

Boats to be let and housed.

J. ROGERSON ; J. ROSEWELL ; GEO. HONE.

Horses for towing, J. ROSEWELL.

Fishing.—At Walton is one of the best pitches for Bream on the Thames, not far from the old wooden bridge that carries the towing-path over the entrance to the back-water ; and, in places all the way to Sunbury Weir, Bream and Barbel are to be found. Chub likewise and Dace exist along the Middlesex shore, whilst now and then Trout make their appearance.

FISHERMEN.

J. ROGERSON ; J. ROSEWELL ; G. HONE.

RAILWAY STATION at Walton (S. W. R., Main Line), about 1¼ miles from the river.

H. W. TAUNT'S Agent at Oatlands: Mr. NORTH, Stationer.

SUNBUR

SUNBURY LOCK, from Walton Bridge, 1 Hampton Ferry, 2 m. o fur. 110 yds. : fal 6 feet : is very slow in emptying.

There is nothing of importance at Sun anything but pretty or antique. The breed the Thames with Trout, &c., close to the The river-keeper, J. MILBOURN, who lives to explain their peculiarities.

SUNBURY STATION (S. W. R., Branch), river.

INNS.

The "Magpie" (see p. 71), the "Whi the "Flower Pot," the "Castle," in Sunbu on the Surrey shore.

Boats housed and to b

*E. CLARK ; *T. and A. STROUD.

Ponies for towing, J. MILBOURN.

Fishing.—Sunbury Weir, with the stre a fine reach for fly-fishing, as well as ho fish. A back-water runs out below the L side, and is good for Dace : lower dow amongst the rod-aits, are Chub and Jack : Works, are Perch and Jack ; whilst when are Roach, Dace, Barbel, &c. Round t abound, and in the back-water, Chub, &c.

Thames River-keeper, J. MILBOURN.

FISHERMEN.

E. CLARK ; T. and A. STROUD.

H. W. TAUNT'S Agent at Sunbury: Mr. R

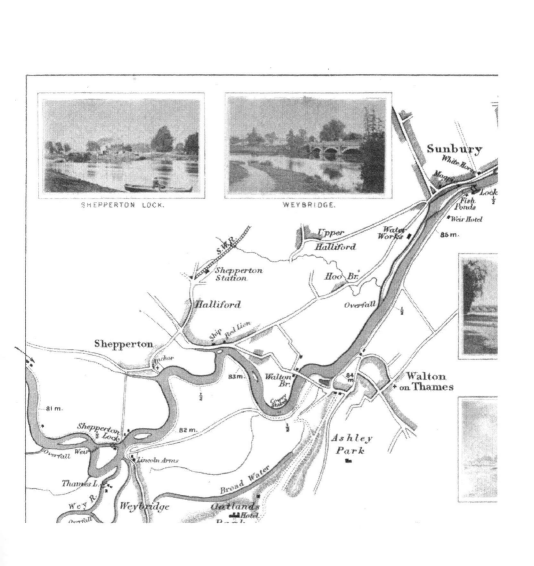

SHEPPERTON LOCK.

WEYBRIDGE.

Sunbury

White Horse

Magpie

Lock

Fish Ponds

Weir Hotel

85 m.

Water Works

Upper Halliford

S.W.R.

Shepperton Station

Hoo Br.

Overfall

Halliford

Ship Red Lion

Anchor

Shepperton

83 m.

Walton Br.

Walton on Thames

81 m.

82 m.

Shepperton Lock

Lincoln Arms

Ashley Park

Overfall Weir

Thames L.

Broad Water

Wey R.

Weybridge

Oatlands

Hotel

Overfall

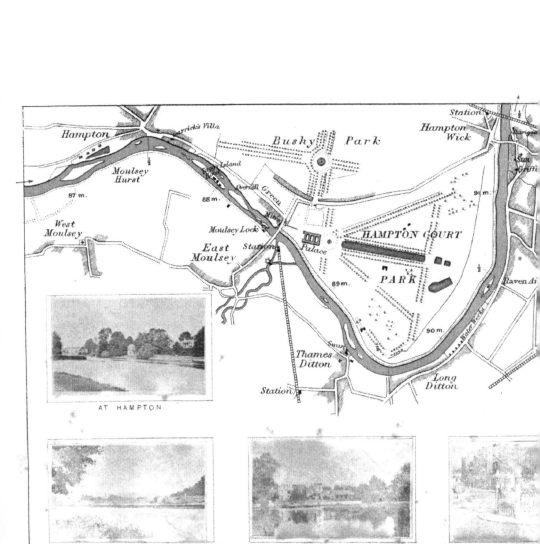

Hampton

Garrick's Villa

Bushy Park

Station

Hampton Wick

Moulsey Hurst

Island

Overall Green

87 m.

West Moulsey

88 m.

Moulsey Lock

East Moulsey

Station

Palace

Mill

91 m.

HAMPTON COURT

PARK

89 m.

½

Raven Ai

90 m.

Water Works

Swan

Thames Ditton

Long Ditton

Station

AT HAMPTON.

HAMPTON.

HAMPTON FERRY, from Sunbury, 2 m. o fur. 110 yds.; to Moulsey Lock, 6 fur. 110 yds.

RAILWAY STATION (S. W. R., Branch), about 1 mile from the river.

HAMPTON is only noted for its races, which take place on what is known as Moulsey Hurst, on the Surrey side of the river. It once had even a more unenviable reputation, when prize-fights and duels were the rage; but these have passed away. The most noticeable house is that in which Garrick lived, after his retirement from the stage. It may be known by the Rotunda standing close to the river, which contained the statue of Shakespeare, now in the British Museum.

Hotel, the " Lion."

INNS.

The " Bell."
The " Crown." (See p. 71.)

Boats to be let and housed.

*BENN and SON.
*J. SNELL.
*J. LANGSHAW.
W. SNELL.
MARY SNELL.
Ponies for towing, DAVID HILL.

FISHERMEN.

BENN and SON.
R. GODDARD.
J. SNELL.
J. LANGSHAW.
W. SNELL.

TAGG'S ISLAND AND

Boats to be let and housed, *T. G. TAGG.

Hotel, " Island Hotel." (See p. 72.)

MOULSEY AND HAMPT(

MOULSEY LOCK, from Hampton Ferry, (Thames Ditton, 1 m. o fur. 209 yds.: falls o 6 feet. There is a boat-launch here, open i boats, to save them going through the Loc series of rollers down an incline, and is o the Lock.

HAMPTON COURT STATION (S. W. R., Bra Bridge, Surrey side.

HAMPTON COURT BRIDGE, just below the picturesque iron structure, which stands in wooden bridge, and connects the village of N Hampton Court. Moulsey has nothing call the palace of Hampton Court must not be p tion being drawn to it. It stands on the Mi distance from the river, and forms a pleasi Surrey shore. Early in the thirteenth cen Hampton Court was bequeathed to the Kni Jerusalem; it remained in their possession the Prior of the order to grant him a lease menced the erection of his palace in 1515. which it was built excited much envy, and le the whole a present to his master, Henry VII

The King accepted the gift, and gave W palace of Richmond. Henry built the grea additions to the buildings, and converted the country round into a chase, which he stocked with deer. Edward VI. was born at Hampton Court. Charles I. was confined here, and tried to make his escape, but failed. William III. pulled down and rebuilt a great part of the palace, under the direction of Sir Christopher Wren; and his death was caused here by his horse stumbling over a mole-hill. Pope immortalized the residence of Queen Anne here, in his poem, "The Rape of the Lock." At present the state apartments, with their rich treasures of art, and the beautiful gardens, are open to the public. The greatest glory of Hampton Court was the collection of cartoons by Raphael, designed to be copied in tapestry for the Sistine Chapel in Rome; they are now in the South Kensington Museum. The gardens, with the celebrated vine, are also objects of attraction; and the fun of being lost in the Maze has helped to brighten many a holiday at Hampton Court.

The river Mole joins the Thames by two mouths at Moulsey.

Boats housed and to be let.

*T. G. TAGG.
R. WATFORD.
G. SIDDINGS.
H. TAGG.
T. TAGG, sen.

HOTELS.

The " Mitre," Hampton Court.
Tagg's Island Hotel, (see under Tagg's Island).
The " Castle."
The " Prince of Wales," Moulsey.

Inn, the " Carnarvon Castle," Moulsey.

Fishing.—Moulsey Weir is noted for its Trout, and good fishing is to be had at Hampton Court Bridge, just below. The water

gallery hole, close under the rails on the t[...] a safe refuge for good Trout; and on the [...] water will repay a cast with the fly. Roac[...] abound all down this reach; and in som[...] are to be found. A fine place for campi[...] land just behind the first little ait below H[...]

FISHERMEN.

WM. MILBOURNE; THOS. DAVIS and S[...] THOS. WHEELER; J. HEDGER; JOHN [...] V. STONE; WM. ROGERSON; C. GRIFFIN; [...]

THAMES DIT[...]

THE " Swan Hotel," at Ditton, has a rep[...] well sustained by its present host. It is a [...] described by Theodore Hook, whose ver[...] recited in the village. The following is a s[...]

> " Here in a placid waking dream
> I'm free from worldly troubl[...]
> Calm as the rippling silver stre[...]
> That in the sunshine bubble[...]
> And, when sweet Eden's blissf[...]
> Some abler bard has writ on [...]
> Despairing to transcend his po[...]
> I'll *ditto* say for *Ditton*."

RAILWAY STATION (S. W. R.), about 4 fur[...]

Hotel, the " Swan."

Boats housed and to be let.

W. Tagg.
J. Tagg.
H. Rogerson.
H. Tagg.

Fishing.—The fishing from here to Kingston is for Trout, moderate; Barbel, good; Roach, Dace, and Gudgeon, exceedingly good.

At Thames Ditton deeps are Jack; and below, along the walls of the Water Works, are heavy Perch.

FISHERMEN.

W. Tagg.
J. Tagg.
H. Rogerson.

At Long Ditton, just below, boats are let by H. Hammerton and B. Buttery; the latter of whom also pursues the occupation of fisherman.

SURBITON.

Soon after leaving Ditton we reach Surbiton, with its favourite promenade along the bank of the river, and rows of pretty villa residences behind; but there is nothing else to attract our attention.

Boats housed and to be let.

*J. Messenger, Raven Ait.
Mrs. Parker, Surbiton Promenade.

The Thames Sailing Club has its head-quarters here.

KINGSTON.

Kingston Bridge, from Thames Ditton, 1 m. 7 fur. 55 yds.; to Teddington Lock, 1 m. 6 fur. 88 yds.

Kingston Railway Station (S. W. R.), a
bridge.

The history of Kingston-on-Thames is it
existed under the Romans; in Saxon times it
still retains the celebrated king's or coronatio
the Saxon kings sat at their coronation.
days has been placed in a favourable spot,
the market-place; and on it is engraved the
nine kings, said to have been crowned here.
coronation of Edwy took place here, and
event which caused the brutal branding
Elfgiva, and the deposition and death of the l
noticed in Domesday Book as a royal deme
owes its first charter. The Church, which w
of Richard II., the market-place and town-h
are the only objects of interest, besides the
tioned. A large market is held here, and
quarters of several rowing clubs, some of whic
in the various regattas held here, and at othe

Boats housed and to be le

*J. Messenger; J. Stevens; *R. Turk
p. 72); *F. Eastland; *C. and A. Burgoyn
Wick, (see p. 72).

Ponies for hire for towing, Mrs. Merrett.

Waterman, J. Smith.

HOTELS.

The "Griffin." (See p. 73.)
The "Sun."

INNS.

The "Outrigger;" the "Anglers;" and the "Ram."

Fishing.—At Kingston, fishing is fully up to the average for Roach, Chub, and Bream; Barbel are to be found near both the bridges; and below the railway bridge, close to the mouth of the sewer, are Roach, with splendid Barbel in a hole close by: Chub line the aits below, where a fly may be thrown with every chance of success; and fine Jack abound all along the reach down to Teddington Weir, just above which, at Rat Island, is a good place for Roach and Perch.

FISHERMEN.

JOHNSON and SONS; WM. CLARK; W. BAGNELL; and JOSEPH STEVENS and SON, Barge Walk Cottage, 3 fur. below the bridge.

TEDDINGTON.

TEDDINGTON LOCK, from Kingston Bridge, 1 m. 6 fur. 88 yds.; to Eel-Pie Island, 1 m. 1 fur. 22 yds.: falls from 6 in. at high tides to 5 ft. 9 in. in low summer water; average in summer, about 5 ft.

RAILWAY STATION (S. W. R.), 5 fur. from the river.

TEDDINGTON LOCK is the last upon the Thames, and is divided into two; the small lock on the left hand being for pleasure-boats. The tide runs up to the Weir, and flows about an hour.

I must call attention here to what I consider an imposition, and warn my fellow-oarsmen that if they cross at the ferry from the Lock side to the village, or *vice versa*, the sum of three-pence will be demanded. The watermen give, as a reason for their charge, the fact that they are under the control of the Waterman's Company, being below Teddington Weir, and that their

rules allow them to do so. This may t does not diminish the imposition of the cas

Boats housed and to be let, *J. MESSENGE *Hotel*, the "Anglers," close to the river. *Inn*, "Royal Oak."

WATERMEN.

HENRY HARRIS; WILLIAM FRANCIS; Jo

FERRY, *(see note above)*

Fishing.—The fishing, below Teddingtor is thoroughly good; as is well attested by punts that ever and anon dot the river dow The favourite spots are the Weir pool, wh force; and just at the bend of the rive where often as many as twenty punts are m

FISHERMEN.

W. KEMP AND SONS; J. KEMP; S. KE BALDWIN; B. STEVENS.

TWICKENHAM, AND
ISLAND.

BETWEEN Teddington and Twickenhar mansions of Strawberry Hill and Pope's V lies back from the water, and is noted fi Walpole, who turned it into a Gothic b stood just above, where the curve of the ri ham begins. It was pulled down by Lad the willow destroyed, that was so well kr by the poet himself. The grotto, I belie a mutilated state.

STAR & GARTER _ RICHMOND.

View from EEL PIE ISLAND.

TEDDINGTON LOCKS.

Station
Marble Hill
Twickenham
Kings Head
Eel Pie I.
94 m.
Strawberry Hill
Ham
Ham Field
Teddington Lock
93 m.
Teddington
Anglers
Teddington Station
S.W.R.

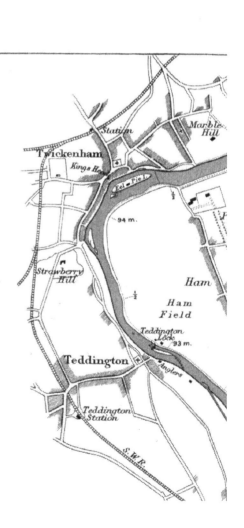

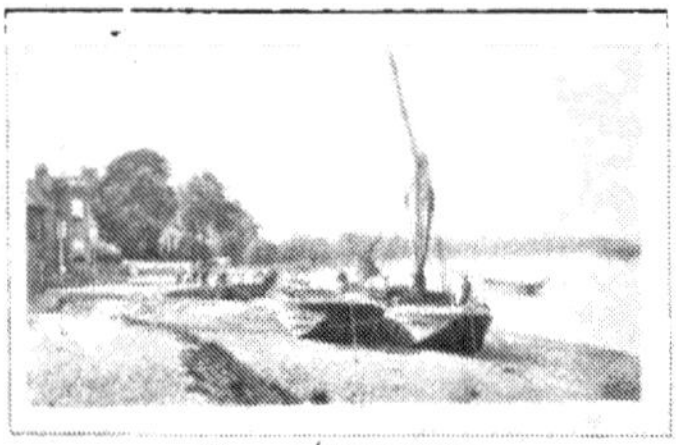

View at MORTLAKE.

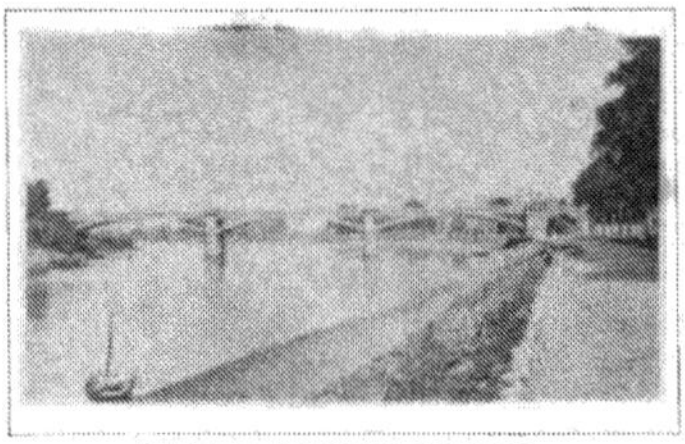

BARNES RAILWAY BRIDGE.

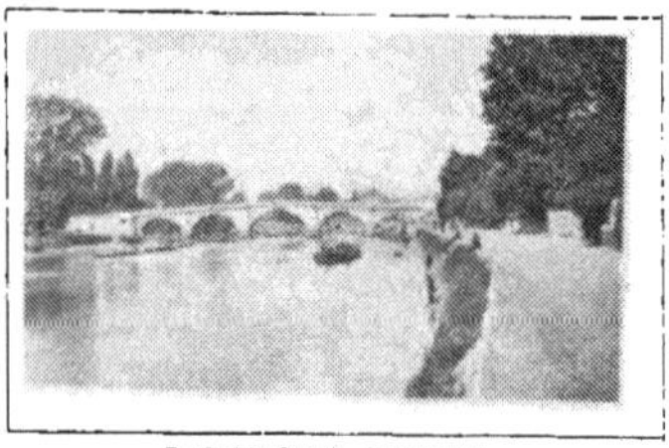

RICHMOND BRIDGE.

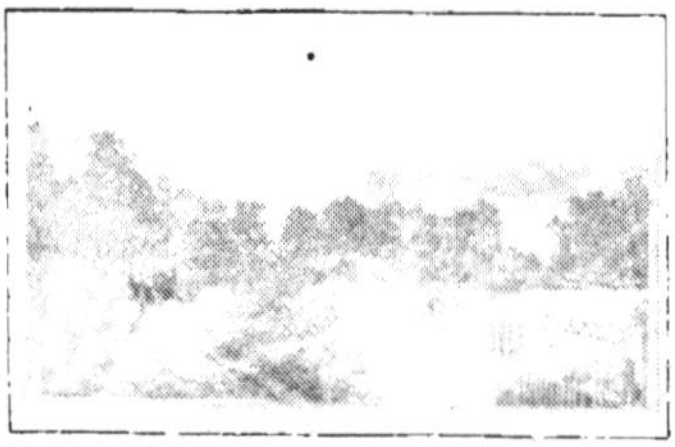

View from RICHMOND HILL.

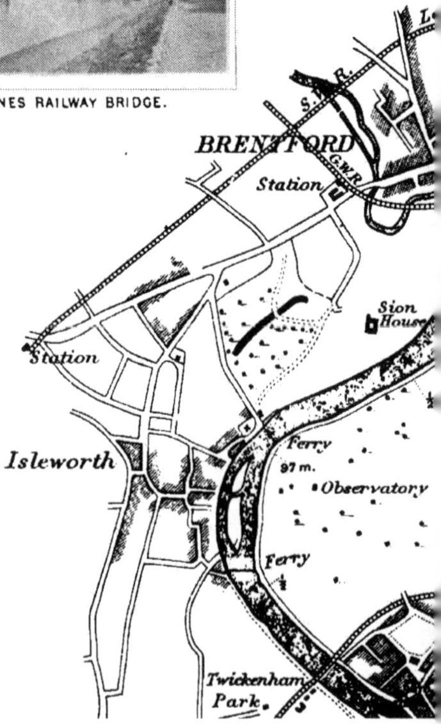
S.W.R.
BRENTFORD
G.W.R.
Station
Sion House
Station
Isleworth
Ferry
97 m.
Observatory
Ferry
Twickenham Park

Eel-Pie Island, just below, is a well-known resort for visitors up the river, and fine views of Richmond Hill, as well as Twickenham, can be obtained from it. Twickenham Church contains the tomb of Pope; but is only interesting from this association, it being an ugly specimen of debased architecture. Just below Twickenham Ferry is the residence of the Princes of Orleans, known by the vases of flowers on the river-wall; and on the opposite side of the river—surrounded with foliage,—is Ham House, the interior of which is said to present an almost unchanged example of a Stuart mansion. The river here is very shallow at low tide, with a swift stream, and the mud-banks will not allow of towing; so that it is always, if possible, better for the oarsman to wait for the tide, than face the rapid current.

HOTELS.

The "White Cross," Eel-Pie Island; the "King's Head," (see p. 74); the "Albany," Twickenham.

INNS.

The "Swan;" the "Queen's Head;" the "Two Sawyers;" and the "George," Twickenham.

Boats to let.

T. COOPER, at the Ferry; J. HAMMERTON; JOHN COXON; E. HAMMERTON; G. COLLIS.

WATERMEN.

G. LEE; C. LEE; H. HAMMERTON; J. HAMMERTON; J. JERDON; W. FRANCIS.

FISHERMEN.

E. FINCH; T. COXON; J. COXON; S. COWELL; T. CHAMBERLAIN; H. CHAMBERLAIN; J. BRAND; S. MESLEY; W. FRANCIS; GEO. COLLIS; RICH. MOFFATT; J. HENNESSEY.

RICHMOND AND PETERSHAM.

PASSING Marble Hill, on the left bank of the river, the views of Richmond gradually unfold their beauty as we float nearer to them. The first place on which our eye rests is the "Star and Garter," a fine building, standing out in a bold position on the brow of the hill, and commanding from its windows the most extensive views. The Duke of Buccleugh's r the river at the corner, on turning which t sight.

RICHMOND BRIDGE, from Eel-Pie Island, : to Kew Bridge, 2 m. 7 fur. 124 yds.: tide flo

RAILWAY STATIONS, L. and S. W. R., and both stations being close together, about 3 fu

RICHMOND, once designated Schene, was, li town. Henry I. had a house here; and s existence are dated at Sheen, during the reigr II.; Edward III. died at the palace in 1377 ; here for part of his reign, and Chaucer was S the palace of Sheen, under him. It was the of Henry VII., who rebuilt the palace, afte fire, and changed the name to Richmond. sionally resided here, and, on Wolsey present ton Court, acknowledged the present by "lic his manor of Richmond at his pleasure." C a prisoner here during part of the reign of : she also inhabited it when queen, and died building fell into decay, and when the Parli the ascendancy, it was partly dismantled. A exists, on the western side of Richmond Gr gateway and a turreted building. According t the room over the gateway is that in which the ham died, after the interview with Elizabeth fessed to having kept back the ring which sentence of death, had entrusted her to de The green was once the favourite jousting days of the palace; and is still used as a But the interest arising from these memori is eclipsed by the natural beauty which unfol the hill: the view from which is one of the river. It has been celebrated in poetry and our best English landscape-painters have imn canvas. The prospect well repays the trou

hill, and the boat can be left at the corner, close to the Duke of Buccleugh's, in care of one of the watermen there, whilst you are gone. When on the hill, pay a visit to the park—enclosed by Charles I.—from which also extensive views are to be obtained. Richmond Bridge is a picturesque structure of five arches, and, being prettily situated, is a great ornament to the river. The poet Thomson lived at Richmond, and wrote several of his poems here; he is buried in the old church.

Boats housed or to be let.
Those marked ' are Boat-builders.

* W. Wheeler and Sons; * E. Redknap; * E. Messam and Son; *H. Redknap; *Searle and Sons; *G. Messam; J. Glover; J. Callis; W. Platt.

Boats housed and to be let (Petersham).

*E. Messam and Son, (Landsdown Boat-house); J. Chitty.

WATERMEN.

C. Wheeler, (in ordinary to the Queen); Wm. Platt; Geo. Platt, sen.; Geo. Platt, jun.; J. Mansell; J. Cann; E. Cripps; J. Borley; Robt. Chitty; Edward Chitty; Alf. Chitty; Jas. Frewen; J. Mackinny; C. Fenn.

HOTELS.

"Star and Garter;" "Castle;" "Talbot;" "Greyhound."

INNS.

"King's Head;" "White Cross;" "Three Pigeons;" "Compasses;" "Old Ship."

Fishing.—The fishing all round Richmond is thoroughly good; and as numerous parties from London and elsewhere visit it, fishermen and punts are to be obtained without much trouble.

FISHERMEN.

H. Mansell; C. Brown; R. New; H. Howard; Wm. Platt; Geo. Platt; H. Wheeler; J. Brain.

H. W. TAUNT'S Agent at Richmond : Mr. COOK, Hill-street.

ISLEWORTH AN[

Leaving Richmond, the river flows on\
side by the fine walk which stretches roun\
dens to the bridge; and on the other, pa\
sions, soon arrives at Isleworth. Islewo\
to boast except the Church tower, the\
being an ugly structure of brick. It o\
to Sion close by. The site of Sion, no\
of the Duke of Northumberland, was a\
the order of St. Bridget, the only one of th\
was suppressed by Henry VIII., who rese\
it was presented by Edward VI. to the P\
after his attainder and execution, to the D\
Lady Jane Grey resided here when the\
the accepting of which led to her death\
when the estate once more reverted to t\
stored by Queen Mary to the Sisters of a\
cially of St. Bridget. Elizabeth, however,\
gave Sion to the Earl of Northumberland,\
remains.

Boats housed and to be

J. Waite, W. Styles, both above the A

INNS.

The "Northumberland;" the "London

WATERMEN.

W. Faulkner; E. Finn.

BRENTFO[

Brentford Station (G. W. R.), close t\
. . . . "Tedio\
For dirty streets and white-legged ch\
Brentford excels, I believe, the celeb\
with its thousand-and-one smells. It is ch\
skirmish between the Royal and Parliam\
in which the former were victorious.

Boats to let at the Ferry, H. Thomas.

KEW AND STRAND-ON-THE-GREEN.

KEW BRIDGE, from Richmond Bridge, 2 m. 7 fur. 124 yds. ; to Barnes Railway Bridge, 2 m. 0 fur. 178 yds. : tide flows, three hours.

KEW STATION (S. W. R.), 2 fur. from the Bridge.

KEW GARDENS border the river on the Surrey shore, and form one of the attractions to London holiday-folk, who come here to spend a day's outing in the beautiful plant-houses, &c. They were *private* pleasure-gardens belonging to the Crown, but during the reign of her present Majesty they have been generously relinquished, and put under the management of the Commissioners of Woods and Forests as public national gardens. They are open free.

STRAND-ON-THE-GREEN lies on the other side of the river, below Kew Bridge, but has no noticeable features. Kew Bridge is of stone ; it was opened in 1790.

Boats housed and to be let.

*F. MAYNARD, Strand-on-the-Green.

*J. WISE ; WILLIAMS and SON, Kew.

HOTELS.

The "Oxford and Cambridge," (see p. 73) ; "Star and Garter." *Inn*, "Rose and Crown."

MORTLAKE.

FROM Kew to Mortlake is a long dreary bit of the Thames, without any object of interest to break up its loneliness, except on such occasions as the Oxford and Cambridge Boat-race, when the river is alive with countless legions of boats of every shape and calibre.

The village of Mortlake was the residence of Dr. Dee, the celebrated astrologer and alchymist in the reign of Elizabeth : he died here, and was buried in the churchyard. Partridge, also, the almanac-maker, whose death was humorously predicted by Swift, and afterwards maintained by argument to be true, also lies here. Mortlake is famous as the site of the first tapestry manufactory in England ; it was set up by Sir Francis Crane in 1619, but did not long prosper. Mortlake owes its notoriety at the present day to

its being the end of the regatta-course, begin: is very different on race-days from the dull q it in ordinary times.

Hotel and landing-place, the "Ship." (See MORTLAKE STATION (S. W. R.), 3 fur. from

BARNES.

BARNES RAILWAY BRIDGE, from Kew, 2 m Hammersmith Bridge, 1 m. 5 fur. 196 yds.: tide BARNES RAILWAY STATION (S. W. R.), on t from the river.

Boats housed.

*E. MAY, at Barnes Bridge ; C. WILLCOX, "

HOTELS.

"White Hart," "Bull's Head," both close

CHISWICK

CHISWICK CHURCH forms a pleasing objec is well known from being the burial-place of painter, as well as of several other persons of House, the seat of the Duke of Devonshir further up the stream, and is known for it which would rank still higher were they not ticultural gardens at hand. The celebrated and George Canning both died here.

Steam Yacht Builder, J. J. THORNYCROFT.

Inn, "Old Red Lion."

Ferry, at high tide, by the Ait.

HAMMERSMI

HAMMERSMITH STATION (Met. Ry.), abc Bridge.

HAMMERSMITH BRIDGE, from Barnes Railwa 196 yds. ; to Putney Bridge, 1 m. 6 fur. 22 yds 3 hrs. 45 min.

PASSING Chiswick Ait, we soon arrive at I the Thames is crossed by a graceful suspensio to the one at Marlow. A short distance stood Brandenburg House, the residence, fo:

fortunate wife of George IV.; she also died here. Soon after her death the house was razed to the ground. Hammersmith Church is a finer building than many we have passed in the latter part of the Thames, and contains a remarkable monument to Sir Nicholas Crispe, supporting a bronze bust of Charles I. In Hammersmith itself is nothing worthy of notice.

Boats housed and to be let.

*BIFFEN and SONS; *E. MAY; —. SAWYER; T. WISE.

HOTELS.

The " Rutland;" the " City Arms."

Inn, " Beaulieu Arms," (Surrey side).

PUTNEY AND FULHAM.

PUTNEY BRIDGE, from Hammersmith, 1 m. 6 fur. 22 yds.; to Wandsworth, about 6 fur.; to London Bridge, about $7\frac{1}{2}$ miles: tide flows, about 4 hrs.

THE river below Hammersmith passes on the right bank Barnes Elms, the residence of Sir Francis Walsingham in the time of Queen Elizabeth; and after him, amongst others, of the poet Cowley. A house close by was the residence of Jacob Tonson, the bookseller; and here the Kit-Cat Club held its meetings, the room being built specially, and hung round with Kneller's famous portraits of the members.

Putney is now well known as the head-quarters of many of the rowing-clubs, and at various seasons, particularly that of the annual training and race of the Oxford and Cambridge Eights, it is the centre of a fashionable gathering. The London Rowing Club has lately erected a fine new boat-house, from which a splendid view of the start and racing for the first mile and a half can be obtained. Putney Bridge is an old structure of wood, very inconvenient, although picturesque. It once existed, that yielded, according to annual toll of twenty shillings to the lor above is the Aqueduct, conveying the wate Water Companies across the Thames.
close to the Bridge, and that of Fulham or river. Tradition says these churches were but no record remains of the fact. Thon here, and also Gibbon, the great historian on his way to Hampton Court, after his di cellorship. At Fulham is the residence of and in the Church are monuments to sever side of the churchyard is bounded by a pic houses; and the Church itself is worth a architectural beauties.

Boats housed and to be

WILLIAM EAST; RICHARD SIMMONS; Jo JOHN PHELPS, Fulham.

HOTELS.

The " Fox and Hounds," (the Oxford Garter," (the Cambridge House); the " W Lion."

INNS.

The " Bells," (Harry Kelly's old house). The " Duke's Head."

Inn at Fulham, " Eight Bells." Omnibus

Steamboats to all the piers on the ri Bridge, run from Putney Pier every half-ho

Parties wishing to proceed to Wandsw house at Salter's, and accommodation at th

H. W. TAUNT'S Agents at Putney: — ROB

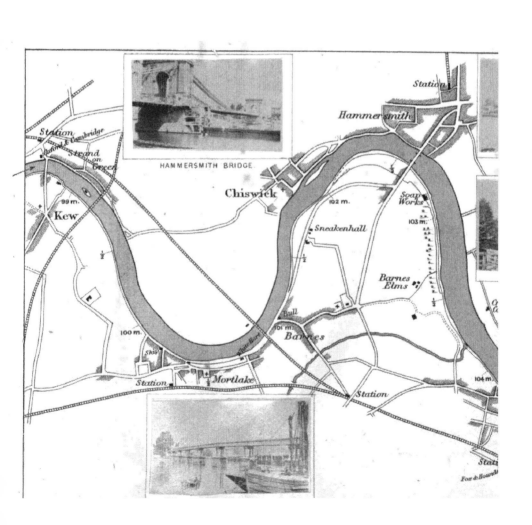

HAMMERSMITH BRIDGE.

Station

Hammersmith

Station

Cambridge

Strand on Green

Chiswick

Soap Works

102 m.

103 m.

99 m.

Kew

Sneakenhall

Barnes Elms

½

½

½

½

Bull

100 m.

Barnes

101 m.

Ship

Station

Mortlake

Station

104 m.

Station

Fox & Hounds

(*Continued from p.* 31.)

on the top, with our carpet-bags at the head, form the mattress, which is made complete by a rug thrown over, and blankets or rugs make up the interior of our sleeping-room. On the outside a line is stretched from mast to mast, and on this is threaded the rings of a waterproof, each end ring being stretched to its mast, and eyelet-holes in each corner fastened to buttons on the boat. Thus we have a water-tight dry sleeping-place, and anything but an uncomfortable one.

I have given the method of preparing the water-tight on p. 51, but should my description not be sufficient, I have a photograph of the boat, shewing the mode of fitting up, amongst both my series of views. Thus far the boat; and another of its advantages is that you can sleep where you like. If you choose to cast anchor, you can sleep in the very centre of the stream, where no one can reach you without a boat, or you can sleep up the smallest ditch that you pass on your journey. I found it a very great advantage to have two short iron rye-pecks, with cords attached to the head and stern of the boat: these moored us to any place, and were very convenient at all times. I need hardly say, do not moor on the tow-path bank, or you may chance to find yourself in a mess from the towing-line of some passing barge catching in your upper works.

Camp Furniture.—Camp furniture need not be very elaborate. A frying-pan, pot, and kettle, all to fit a fireholder, will be all that are really required, with the usual plates, mugs, &c., that each one will use; but in every case, if you are camping out, *don't take more than you can help.* You will be surprised how many things you can do without; a wicker-basket will hold your pot, &c., with the necessary fuel for burning, and the other things will go with the food into your locker.

Fuel.—Wood is to be bought everywhere in the country, but if a wheelwright or carpenter's shop is handy, try there first. A hatchet will be necessary, to chop it up with.

Matches.—Keep your matches dry. We h⸺ last summer for some, and to wait two hou⸺ a hard day's work, through letting them get w⸺

Food.—"Nothing like leather" used to be ⸺ we had beef; and sometimes it was a puzzle, not begun, to know whether it was tender ⸺ like leather" was used to express either. I⸺ beef-steak, cooked either over the coals or ⸺ camping out; and this often formed the *pièce* ⸺ dinner after a stiff day's work. Usually, we h⸺ (just after our bathe—a thing which helps ⸺ much,) and made a good meal; in the mi⸺ feasted on a crust and cheese, and washed it ⸺ of "home-brew'd," kept for that purpose in ⸺ failing that, a glass of Thames water, qualifi⸺ some concentrated milk. When we reached ⸺ ground, (we usually moved every day,) we ma⸺ dinner ready, taking tea with it; and a glass ⸺ a biscuit, sent us to bed about nine o'clock at ⸺ tioned before, there are a lot of portable thing⸺ are uncommonly useful in camping out. T⸺ from Australia are included in these, as well a⸺ viands, &c., that are in universal request. A⸺ be eaten cold just as it is, with a little sauce t⸺ some salad can be got at, a fair dinner or l⸺ with but little trouble; and then the variou⸺ may be cooked would fill a chapter as long ⸺ only give you one. Wash and scrape some p⸺ slice them up, with some onions, and boil ti⸺ meat in *quantum suff.;* leave for a few minu⸺ vour, and serve. The Australian meats al⸺ soups, are not much trouble, and, when yo⸺ meat, come in very useful, so much so that we⸺

as a reserve. Tea, sugar, butter, and all those sort of things, we kept in tin biscuit-boxes, easily procured at the grocers. These are always clean, and do not let the things get wet. A ham, too, for "rashers for breakfast," is not a bad thing to keep, and the concentrated milk—or that with chocolate—must not be forgotten. Of course, every one must form his own ideas on a subject like this, so I have only indicated those things most essential.

Clothing.—An extra suit in a *soft* bag should be taken, in case of wet weather or any other mishap, as well as to be able to change for sleeping at night. Also, of course, the toilet requisites, but not too many of them. The few things I take in that way afford matter for a standing joke with one of my friends; but one doesn't require to spend an hour twice a-day preparing for meals and "parade," when camping out. I spoke of a *soft* bag, as you will require it for a pillow; but if you prefer to use a stiff portmanteau, of course you are at liberty to do so; only, don't blame me, if your sleep is not so sound as it might be. And that brings me to another point, and one of the most important,—

Sleeping.—If you don't sleep well, you will not enjoy yourself; and this is why I so much prefer my boat to a tent. We have always a *dry* sleeping apartment. Last summer was a wet one, and I think more rain fell in one week than we had for nine weeks in the summer before, yet we had no difficulties on account of the rain, as far as sleeping was concerned, but when the wet came on, generally took shelter in bed, or in the daytime moved the middle boards, and read, or wrote, or talked, under our awning, as it pleased us most. Only on one occasion did the rain inconvenience us, when the water had risen above the britton-boards, and my man, in hurriedly turning out of bed in the morning, put his foot into it, which he sharply drew back with a shocking exclamation. Ugh! In a tent this inconvenience arises; if the ground is at all sloping, the water runs down the

side of the tent, and underneath you, so sleep on water-tight cloth, the damp must extent. I see fellows with camp-bedste them from the damp, but I think if their for once as a sleeping-place they would care of themselves.

Ladies have the idea that sleeping on "Arn't you afraid to go to sleep, in case is the question generally asked. "No, ne one, and if all three were to roll down o done), it would not even dip." Ladies d the limited space renders it inconvenien a toilet; but I may tell you I have know in a boat like mine, and thoroughly en after camping out all day, go and sleep at of delicate persons perhaps this is wise; prepared for sleeping out at all times. have a stiff day's pulling, and when fairly only Inn in the village, and be told there "No, sir; we are crammed; havn't a roo that another, at four or five miles distance are bent on trying for the accommodati uncertainty whether you will get it. Th happens, and always when you are most for it; but if you camp, you just make y like,—the fire is lit, the steak fried, and, v toes straight from the pot, is relished as o does relish food. The beef-steaks have potatoes or cabbage, (quite fresh, perhaps previously,) have a crisper taste than they

But I am running away from my subjec are running away with me, and this won't turn again. "How did you sleep?" is asked of a guest who has passed the night under your roof; but in camping out one scarcely ever knows even when he does go to sleep, or recollects anything after rolling himself in his rug, till the morning light peeping through his eyelids rouses and tells him it is time to rise; and then how pleasant the tumble-out of bed, and into the fresh, clear stream; a good rub down and an exhilarating run making one ready to eat a good donkey-steak, if nothing more was to be had.

And now a word on cooking and buying things. "It's no use my camping out, I can't cook," says one. Don't tell me, but try it; you will soon learn. What, not able to cook a beef-steak or chop, boil some potatoes or cabbage, and get up a plain dinner? Well, you are the very person who ought to camp out; it will teach you self-reliance. If you are afraid of the cooking, get your wife or your sweetheart to shew you how; don't be ashamed to learn, even from them; you won't find much difficulty about it. And then, as to buying. Bread and meat are better had fresh every morning, if possible, as they both get stale very quickly; and the stone jar, which holds enough for the day, filled at the nearest

Inn; (don't take too much, particularly in th the better). Of the other things a stock had replenished whenever getting short, before the

If a party of two or three are together, let own part,—one do the buying, one the cook division of labour is always an advantage, an own part best. But I find I have got past the so must end by telling you if you cannot ge take dinner with us; and then you will see fc five minutes than I can tell you in a hour. I an elegant dinner; but if a good plain one wil I shall be very pleased to see you. We don' but keep rice, which is easily carried: it make dings, easily cooked, and very palatable. a glass to ask a fellow-camper-out to, and som of grog to wet a pipe with in the evening. S you will be made welcome by

Yours very t

HOW TO PREPARE A WATER-TIGHT SHEET.

GET some good duck, and have it sewn together to the size required, with each seam lapped (making two rows of stitching to each seam), the edge turned in all round, and the eyelets inserted; then, hanging it up by the corners, wet it with water and let it get drained (not dry): after this well brush into it some *boiled* oil (linseed), which will lather with the water, and let it hang in the open air a day or two to carefully over again with *raw* oil, and leave will find your sheet thoroughly water-tight, an good. If damaged at any time, a fresh coat make good.

INDEX TO ADVERTISEMENTS.

THE BEETLE AND WEDGE,

MOULSFORD FERRY.

(Close to the River on the right bank.)

GOOD ACCOMMODATION FOR TOURISTS, ANGLERS, &c.

BOATS HOUSED, OR TO BE LET.

Fishing-punts and Fishermen.

S. SWADLING, *Proprietor.*

THE SWAN INN,

STREATLEY, BERKS.

(Close to the River on the right bank.)

GOOD ACCOMMODATION FOR TOURISTS, ANGLERS, &c.

BOATS HOUSED, BUILT, OR TO BE LET.

Fishing-punts and Fishermen.

C. SAUNDERS, *Proprietor.*

THE BULL I

STREATLEY, BER

J. GARDINER, Proprietor.

This House, being delightfull
the foot of the beautiful Hills,
accommodation to parties visit

Splendid Ales on draug.
SUPERIOR WINES AND S
Well-aired Beds.

W. FORD,

ELEPHANT & CASTL

PANGBOURNE, BE

Close to the Railway and River T

Gentlemen and Families visiting this
will find every Accommodation at Mode
W. FORD is the Lessee of the Fishing
above the weir down to Mr. Powys' at
description on Map, under Pangbourne.)

RAY MEAD HOTEL

BOULTER'S LOCK,

Near Maidenhead Bridge,

W. DEACON, *Proprietor.*

BEAUTIFULLY SITUATE ON THE BANKS OF THE THAMES.

ROOMS AND APARTMENTS.

HENRY WOODHOUSE,

Boat and Punt Builder,

THE LIMES, BRAY,

AND AT THE RAY MEAD HOTEL.

Pleasure Boats and Punts of every description Built to Order, with latest Improvements.

Waterman by Appointment to the Queen.

T. G. TAGG,

BOAT BUILDER,

ISLAND BOAT-HOUSE,

EAST MOULSEY,

AND

HAMPTON COURT,

Begs to inform the Rowing public that he has now increased his business on the Island by erecting an Hotel adapted for every accommodation required by them. Gentlemen will find the Hotel and Boat-houses as conveniently situated as any on the River Thames for Hiring or Housing Boats, being above the Lock at Moulsey, and only forty minutes' ride from Waterloo Station; five minutes' walk from Hampton Court Station, and fifteen from Teddington through Bushey Park. The Island is also specially laid out for Anglers, where they can insure a good day's Fishing; it is five acres in extent, and situated in the middle of the Thames Angling Preservation Society's Hampton Preserves.

T. G. TAGG also undertakes to build Boats, Punts, and Canoes of every description; and by employing the best workmen and material he hopes to give the same satisfaction he has done for the last ten years. By his general knowledge of the Trade, and personal superintendence of the work, he is able to turn out superior craft, such as have been so highly recommended for up-river work for the last few years.

Boats for Hire by Season, Month, or Week.

Masts, Sails, Sleeping and Excursion Tents made to order, and Boats' Gear of every description.

Private Boats Repaired and Varnished.

BOATS CARTED TO ANY PART OF THE THAMES.

Depôt of the Canoe Club, where Members' Canoes are housed free.

C. & A. BURGOIN

CENTRE-BOARD YACHT AND BO

KINGSTON-ON-THA

Near the Griffin Hotel and Market-

And Lower Teddington-road, Ha

Adjoining the Railway Bridge.

C. and A. B. respectfully call the attention of th world to their improved Centre-board Rowing and S coast or river use, thus rendering sailing an attainm found in rowing-boats. Workmanship and materials best quality.

Their improved Centre-board when affixed to yacht the cabin accommodation.

Boats of every Description Built on the

Photographs may be had on applica

BOATS HOUSED, &c.

CHARLES MELS

BOAT BUIL

Near the Bridge,

KINGSTON-ON-THAME

BOATS CAREFULLY HOU

Boats and Punts for Angling, for

OATLANDS PARK HOTE

WALTON-ON-THAMES, SURREY.

ONE HOUR FROM LONDON BY RAILWAY—WATERLOO

FOR FAMILIES AND GENTLEME

Magnificent private Park of 36 Acres, beautifully Timbered, and
most extensive Views over the Valley of the Thames

Visitors are received on fixed Weekly Charges, or by

Post-Horses, and excellent Open or Close Carriag

Prospectus and Tariff on application to Mr.

Now Ready, price 2s. 6d.

A POCKET EDITION OF THIS

MAP AND GUIDI

TO

THE THAMES.

The Maps reproduced by Photo-Lithogr

(ON A SCALE OF ONE INCH TO THE MILE

FROM THIS TWO-INCH MAP,

Combined with a corresponding Itinerary, giving full descriptions and every information required by

THE OARSMAN, THE TOURIST, AND THE ANGLI

OXFORD: HENRY W. TAUNT, 33, CORNMARKET-STREET.

Lightning Source UK Ltd.
Milton Keynes UK
UKHW020729210121
377450UK00006B/647

9 781376 363708